IN SICKNESS AND IN HEALTH

IN SICKNESS
&IN HEALTH
A LOVE STORY

KAREN PROPP

RODALE

Note: Names of some people in this book have been changed to protect their privacy.

Printed in the United States of America
Rodale Inc. makes every effort to use acid-free ∞, recycled paper ♻.

Cover design by Joanna Williams

Library of Congress Cataloging-in-Publication Data

Propp, Karen.
  In sickness & in health : a love story / Karen Propp.
    p.   cm.
  ISBN 1–57954–552–1 hardcover
  1. Propp, Sam—Health. 2. Prostate—Cancer—Patients—United States—Biography. I. Title: In sickness and in health. II. Title.
  RC280.P7 P737   2002
  362.1'9699463'0092—dc21   2002002576

Distributed to the book trade by St. Martin's Press

2 4 6 8 10 9 7 5 3 1   hardcover

Visit us on the Web at www.rodalestore.com, or call us toll-free at (800) 848-4735.

WE **INSPIRE** AND **ENABLE** PEOPLE TO IMPROVE
THEIR LIVES AND THE WORLD AROUND THEM

For my husband and son

ACKNOWLEDGMENTS

My deepest thanks go first to Laureen Rowland, at David Black Literary Agency, for her tireless and inspired efforts in bringing this book to light. She read every draft with keen insight, offered unstinting encouragement, and eased the work with her good humor and ready laughter.

To the members of my longstanding writers' group: Lauren Slater, as always, was a fount of writerly sustenance; Pagan Kennedy offered much good advice; Tehila Lieberman was an astute reviewer; Sue Resnick, Susan Mahler, Nadine Boughton, and Harvey Blume gave thoughtful readings throughout. Thanks to Lise Stern for suggesting the title.

To Stephanie Tade, whom I am lucky to have as my editor at Rodale. Her vision and generosity made this book what it is. Thanks also to Chris Potash at Rodale for his patience and care with the manuscript.

To the many health care professionals who helped my husband and me during the years described in this book: Dr. Alex Althausen, Dr. Amy Brager, Dr. Irwin Goldstein, Dr. Michael Kane, Dr. Philip Kantoff, Dr. Uriel Meshoulam, Terry Payton, R.N., Dr. Peter Scardino, Dr. William Shipley, Dr. Leonard Solomon, Dr. Harold Tsai, and Dr. Lori Wroble.

To the members of the Longwood Medical Prostate Cancer Support Group, an affiliation of Us Too International, and particularly Stan Klein, cofounder and patient facilitator.

To the Cambridge Arts Council and the Massachusetts Cultural Council, for partial support while writing this book.

Acknowledgments

To Ann and Preston Browning, the gracious proprietors of Wellspring Writers' Retreat, for providing a quiet space when I needed it most.

Finally, to my husband, my son, my parents, my sister, my brother, and my Aunt Gerdy. They lived this story with me and then lived again with my having to write it all down.

CONTENTS

PROLOGUE: PARIS, 1997

The July we suspect that my husband's prostate cancer has returned, I am seven months pregnant. We go to Paris. Late at night, we walk the dark, lit-up streets to forget that Sam might soon die.

We fashion a schedule to accommodate idleness. We rise at about ten, bathe, dress, breakfast in the hotel's country-curtain dining room. Each day we set out for a different section of the city, to wander and see the sights. Midafternoon, we return to our hotel and sleep. By early evening, we are out again, traveling by Metro to one of Sam's guidebook restaurants, where dining takes several hours.

We put our faith in French cuisine. Food, we hope, will impart divine curative powers. Food, we tell ourselves, is better than sex.

We take the Metro to Alain Ducasse. A photo of me standing beneath the art nouveau station arch in the 16th *arrondissement* shows me wearing a black sequined dress. My belly is tremendous. I am gripping the wrought iron rail as if on a sinking ship.

At the restaurant, tuxedoed waiters seat us at a round mahogany table in a room painted with trompe l'oeil book-filled bookcases. We discuss; we confer; we advise. That's the thing about Sam and me: We use up our decision-making capacities on momentous choices like whether to have truffled potato soup with leeks or tart of young lettuces and tomato confit.

I take a photograph of Sam at the end of that rigorous dining experience. He slumps lazily in his chair, his legs spread in repose, his starched napkin flung casually on his lap, an easy grin on his bearded face. Neither a big nor a small man. A nice-looking one. He has the spry body of a wrestler, which he was in high school. The wineglass before him is empty. He looks rakish and ravaged.

Our last meal in Paris is at a restaurant called Arpege. More than the Picasso museum or the Opera or the shops along the Champs-Élysée, Sam wants to experience Arpege. "Who knows when I'll be here again," he says a little ominously.

Sam could describe for you what we ate. The herb-encrusted pigeon; the beet glaze splattered like paint. The tray complete with a *fromage* from every province, a regular tour of the French countryside, complete with bleating goats and milk cows and intoxicating fields of lavender. The tomato, which arrives squashed as a baked apple, for dessert. "Taste it," Sam directs me. "Have you ever tasted anything like this?"

I hadn't. But what I will remember most about this spectacular meal is the boy at the table next to ours.

He is fourteen and has the well-bred, well-dressed look of a child dining in an expensive adult establishment. He has the tall, gangly frame of an adolescent who is good at sports. He sits closest to his father, with whom he shares glossy hair and long eyelashes, and every once in a while I notice a silent glance pass between them in response to something his mother says.

And then I have trouble seeing him at all. A hard knocking behind my eyes blurs this image.

I too will soon have a boy. And sitting in that fine restaurant, drinking the first wine of my pregnancy, the emotions I've tried to keep in check hit full force. Fourteen more years is a long time for Sam to survive prostate cancer, that much I know. Most medical studies are not nearly so optimistic; they compile mortality rates five, seven years out. The knocking travels to the back of my skull and down my spine. I feel the baby kick my heart. How would I explain an absent father to a boy of fourteen? To a child not yet born?

I excuse myself from the table and am practically ushered to the ladies' room by a cadre of waiters. I splash cold water from a silver faucet on my face. I do not want to cry. Not here, not now. This is my happy time with Sam. Tomorrow we will fly home to Cambridge, and soon enough we will sit in specialists' offices. We will discuss Sam's rising PSA. Sam will go for his biopsy. Soon the baby will arrive. Soon enough events will tumble one after the other, quickly transforming our lives.

I am then suddenly overcome with the enormity of what I've taken on. I've told very few people about Sam's probable cancer recurrence and just now I want someone else to help shoulder the burden. Someone to say, "It'll be all right." Someone to say, "This is how it happened to me." But there is no such someone. No one I know. No friend of a friend. Not even a book to which I can turn.

In such a desolate moment my book begins.

I wash my face in the Arpege ladies' room and walk back on shaky legs to my husband. He smells fresh and fragrant, like the giant calla lilies in a glass vase on the entrance table. He's had his gastronomical experience, drunk plenty of wine. Just then, unafraid to die, he opens his warm hand to me. "Come," he says. "It's time we got going."

It is a balmy, starry night on the rue de Varenne. Our soft-soled shoes are silent on the cobblestone. Sam's hand is a gentle pressure on the small of my back. Gone is my despair, and in its place, a momentary fullness. I am full with food, full with child, and just now, I am full with love for my Sam. Even if everything that follows is disastrous, I tell myself, I have this fullness.

The next morning, we board the flight home. Ahead of us lies a long trip. Savoring this final indolence, I rest my head on Sam's shoulder and for the thousandth time I think how unfair it is that my seemingly healthy husband carries a fatal disease and may well submit to a major operation, one which will seriously lower the quality of his life as well as mine.

Sam rests his hand on my belly to feel the baby move. I'm carrying a new and boisterous life, my skin and hair glow in anticipation, my heart swells. Inside me, the baby's cells divide and divide again, just as they should: fingernails, nostrils, brain. Inside Sam, cells are dividing too, just as they should not.

Sam did not die. Prostate cancer is slow moving and so often treatable that the disease is not a dramatic death sentence rife with bodily horrors, but a survival course studded with disappointment and physical challenge. Prostate cancer complicates aging and compromises marriage. The disease and its aftermath have become a part of our relationship and family, a third party that demands its own time, energy, and attention. In return, this uninvited guest called prostate cancer, whom I know too well, has given me reinventions of sex, marriage, and love—some might say a reinvention of life's core.

PART 1

THE EARLY YEARS

"We were sick of being single; we were terrified of being alone; we were happy together in bed; we were frightened of the future; we were married one day before Bennett had to leave for Fort Sam Houston."

—Erica Jong, Fear of Flying

1

COURTSHIP

Sam and I meet in a time before his cancer, which is also a time before e-mail and cell phones became household items. We meet in Cambridge, Massachusetts, a place where people in the late 1980s pursue advanced degrees with the hope of working to solve world hunger or study quantum mechanics out of sheer fascination.

I meet Sam during the time in my life when I want, more than anything, to settle down, get married, have kids—this despite or because of my two advanced degrees in English, my vagabond years, my feminist upbringing. I am thirty-two. My hair is brown. I have the kind of figure that used to be called statuesque.

When we meet, at a party, he extends a hand in greeting. "Delighted." His voice is arch, playful.

"You know Mitchell," I say. Mitchell is my colleague at the University of Lowell, where I am an instructor. Mitchell told me that Sam works at MIT, lives in Somerville, and is a widower. "He has ontological depth," Mitchell told me. "You won't be bored."

"Who doesn't know Mitchell?" Sam asks now in a mock-serious voice that dissipates the awkwardness at us being set up and simultaneously fans the flirtation flame.

I laugh, a nervous, tinkling, appreciative laugh, as I laugh at so many jokes made by eligible men, my laughter saying, *Maybe this one.*

He offers to refresh my drink, a gin and tonic in a Dixie Cup. I am standing in Miranda's bedroom, four walls partitioned off from a loft. The room is crowded with guests who lounge on Miranda's red Turkish pillows and on her mahogany-carved bed, everyone schmoozing and drinking, an articulate, close-knit, expansive group who have gathered, at various people's homes, for the past ten years, one Friday a month for potluck Shabbat dinners.

This is my first time meeting Miranda, my first time at a Friday night potluck. I was invited by Mitchell, one of the core group, as is Sam, who's been attending for the past five years, ever since he lost his wife.

Miranda greeted me warmly at the door: "Oh, the writer. Mitchell told me about you." Then she flounced off, pulled into conversation by a man with a ponytail.

I study Miranda's room now. Mitchell told me that Miranda is an immigration lawyer. She flies to D.C. for meetings to argue government policy, and this impresses me, accustomed as I am to unemployed poets half-seriously calling themselves the legislators of the world. I have never been in a room quite like this before, one where the ethnic jewelry and the books about social justice and the scent of French perfume combine to portray a single woman who can both enjoy herself and be serious about life.

In truth, meeting Sam here tonight is something rare.

One year ago, I moved back to Boston from Salt Lake City, where I earned, of all things, a Ph.D. in poetry. In Utah, I realized, at a late age, just how much of a Northeast liberal intellectual I really am. Church, gambling, camping . . . those pursuits left me cold. I was viscerally homesick for bagels, bookstores, for people who talked with their hands. For self-preservation, I worked at a station that called itself Radio Free Utah because it dared to broadcast NPR. I returned to Boston to meet Sam or someone like him: someone who does not find me strange, as did the Mormons, for having education instead of children and dark unruly hair instead of a blond shiny coif.

Meeting Sam tonight is rare because I see how easily I could have stayed in Utah and *not* met him. I see how I could have taken a teaching job in North Dakota and forever been the odd number at faculty dinner parties, desperately lonely and dedicated to my job. These were not fears of being single. This was a knowledge of who I am.

Sam and I leave the party together, and down on the dark street he asks for my phone number.

"Lovely to meet you," he says. He stuffs the scrap of paper into his back pocket.

"Yes, lovely."

We stand under the marigold streetlight and, really, at this moment we could be any two people alone in the city, looking.

I live in a large, rambling Victorian house in Jamaica Plain that I share with two painters, Larry and Christine. The dining room has elaborately carved wood moldings, the kitchen floor slants, and the storm windows rattle. We have parties, with jug wine and more painters and writers and carpenters who read philosophy.

Christine's boyfriend comes over every Saturday and sometimes Wednesday. Larry slinks away to stay with his current girlfriend, only to return days later with a vague, distracted air. I have dates. Occasionally one stays over but in the harsh morning light he invariably becomes a stranger.

After the party, I consider calling Sam. But then he calls me. "Hello," he booms. "I'm starting a trope-of-the-month club. This month it's metonymy." I laugh at his absurdity. "You poets, you like only metaphor," he chides. Sam rattles on about how just the other day he was reading Anna Akhmatova in the original Russian, about attending a recent Adrienne Rich poetry reading. Trying to impress me. A computer scientist who can talk his way around literature.

Are you going to hear the lecture on the Middle East at Harvard?

I haven't really thought about it. When?

Don't bother. The guy's a reactionary.

Had I heard the latest on the stolen Vermeer paintings at the Gardner museum?

I had.

Did I know anything about the new Davios restaurant in Brookline Village?

I did not.

Let's try it sometime, he says. Lunch?

At the restaurant, I stare at his hands. They are medium-size, almost small, with hair. Sturdy hands. Square-shaped hands, rather like my own.

Those hands tap the menu. "Let's see, the fresh mozzarella and beefsteak tomatoes sprinkled with basil and olive oil looks good," he says. "I suggest you try the shrimp and crabmeat risotto, their signature piece. And I will have, let's see, what looks good, I will have the shredded chicken and capers basted in red wine." To the waiter, he adds: "And afterward, one white chocolate mousse, two spoons, please."

I am and am not used to a man who takes such control of the menu, one who is so willing to pay for an elaborate meal. In Salt Lake City, I went out once with a Mormon. For someone like me, who went to college in the 1970s, when a date consisted of going to a boy's room and smoking a joint, this evening was enlightening from an anthropological point of view. My Mormon was so orthodox in his dating form that he insisted I wait in my car seat until he came around and opened the passenger door. At first I protested—"I can do it myself!" But he persisted, and then I tuned in to the subtle erotics of this act: my ankles swinging prettily from his low-slung Mustang, the warmth of his hand on mine as he helped me to the pavement.

Before I lived in Utah, I might have argued with Sam's taking charge of the menu. But now, but now . . . have I been nudged toward a more traditional mating dance? Or is it the problem of poetry? I mean, the problem of poetry's inability to make the mortgage payments and the doctor bills. I'm no Emily Dickinson stuck in her room; what's worse, I'm not the academic I once thought I might be. I have a choice; I can do other things. I have skills in addition to writing iambic hexameters. For example: cooking, cleaning, and taking care of children.

During lunch, Sam talks about the work he is doing at the MIT artificial intelligence laboratory. "We're trying to map rhetorical recurrences," he says. "The duration, word count, and text difficulty of speech utterances within a party of two. If we can compile a database large enough to cover every possible conversational instance . . ."

Beneath his suave restaurant manners and ruddy good looks, I see the brainy, awkward Bronx High School of Science guy. He is not the brooding, artistic type I usually fall for. More than attractive, I find him amusing. He is light and dry, like the Chardonnay we sip. More than amusing, I find him familiar.

Familiar because my father is a mathematician more comfortable with numbers than with people. At department parties, he and his colleagues stood in a circle, hands stuffed in their trouser pockets, and stared at the floor until one ventured to comment on an obscure branch of number theory. These men— court wizards with conical hats—fascinated me.

After lunch, Sam suggests a walk. It is a day between winter and spring, a day marked by a brisk wind and a bit of bright sun. "Jamaica Pond," I say, "is beautiful this time of year."

I guide him past the little shops at the end of Harvard Street and across Route 9. I am wearing over-the-ankle lace-up boots and an emerald-colored swing coat. Sam walks beside me in an olive green raincoat, the kind with a removable lining. We fall easily into step. The cold makes us walk quickly. At the pond, weeping willows break up the ice, the forsythia is about to bud—I have the sense that Sam and I are striving toward some destination.

We are halfway around the pond. "Did Mitchell tell you about my wife?" Sam asks, abruptly.

"He said she died in a terrible way. Was it cancer?"

"Leukemia." The name of the disease sounds too loud among the quiet trees.

"What was it like?" I want to know. No one I'd been close to had ever been terminally ill. Sam's experience seems richer than mine.

"You start bargaining," he says. "First, you bargain for a cure, or remission. Then you bargain for a good response to treatment. Then all you want is for the pain to lessen. In the end, there's nothing left to bargain for."

He is angry, his voice gruff, more raw than I'd expect someone to be five years after.

"How did she find out she had it?"

"Her first prenatal blood test. We were happy for exactly one day, the day we found out she was pregnant. The next day, they called with the news of an abnormal white blood count."

"And the baby?"

"The fetus," he corrects. "Aborted immediately. Had to start the chemo right away. In six months, Andrea . . . Andrea was gone."

"Why so quick?"

"The doctors killed her," he mutters. "Wrong chemo doses. Botched liver biopsy that left her to bleed to death internally. Sped up her death. I'd have sued except I didn't want any more pain."

We are nearing the little path that will take us back to the main road. I don't know what to say. Listening to Sam, I feel young, carefree, as if I have my whole life ahead of me. But I also feel young and careless, as if I've wasted precious time.

We go to one movie, two dinners, and at the end of our third lengthy phone conversation, I ask: "Do you want to come to dinner at my house this Saturday?"

Come Saturday, I tidy up the common rooms. Into a cast iron pot I throw chopped onions and garlic, fresh basil, a can of diced tomatoes, and strips of boneless chicken. I fill a five-quart pot with water to boil for the linguine.

"Cooking something up?" teases my housemate Larry. He leans over the stove. He's spruced up for going out: slicked back hair, suede jacket. "You know my rule about how long to wait before the big night? Four dates or forty dollars, whichever comes first."

"Remind me never to go out with you."

And then Larry is gone, and Christine gone too, the putt-putt of her Chevy Nova starting up as she sets off, as she has nearly every Saturday night for the past nine years, to meet Charlie for a $12.95 Special at Doyles.

Sam rings the doorbell at 7:45. He wields a single bird-of-paradise, bright orange, Crayola red.

Sam sniffs his way into the kitchen. "Ah, creative pasta," he says, looking into my pot. "Artistic types do creative things with pasta."

I blush, feeling pegged, found as nothing more or less than an artistic type.

Tonight, as we eat and drink in the darkened dining room, chaperoned by the bird-of-paradise, Sam tells stories about our mutual friend Mitchell's ex-girlfriend, now moved to Maine to work with midwives after the success of her university press book, whose thesis, he explains, argues for the de-medicalization of birth; about how Miranda met her boyfriend, the first in nine years, while waiting in line with Sam at the MIT Media Lab to get tickets for Todd Machover's opera; about an old friend who left the yeshiva in Jerusalem and became a Rolfer in London. Everyone he talks about seems to be experiencing a major swerve or change of course; something I will recognize later as middle age but now see as part of my fascination with Sam.

Although I don't know it at the time, I, too, am ending one portion of my life—a long, contracted post-graduate, post-adolescent, post-poetic portion—and just beginning a gradual turn in which I will tour the grim terrain of disease, the sorry land of limitation, and the difficult place in between called compromise. In other words, I am paddling upstream toward midlife.

In my house, the cat circles once, twice, before curling into the armchair's upholstered seat. A cold spring night rattles a window, loose at its sash. I get up from the table. Sam gets up from the table. I stand, a plate in each hand, watching Sam take one step, two steps, three steps, closing the distance between us. And then he kisses me with his wine-stained mouth.

We clear off the table and bring the dishes into the kitchen. I stand at the tall porcelain double sink and he comes up behind me, puts his arms and then the length of his body against mine. I turn around, wipe my hands on my thighs, and we kiss longer this time, pulling closer and closer until our clothing seems superfluous, something to be shed.

"Would you like to go upstairs to my room?" I say.

I take his hand, lead him up the creaky staircase. I turn on my floor lamp, an old, unsightly thing I painted with bright acrylic reds and pinks—its light makes a muted circle against the wide, scuffed boards of my pine floor.

What can I tell you about this first time, when everything still works? His touch is skillful and I am trembling. His skin is a furnace whose warmth I crave. He is all one piece, a long, flowing line that I want to follow. He brings a condom and I say Yes, yes, yes.

Of that first year we knew one another, what do I remember? I remember shoveling snow together, digging out our cars from under six-foot drifts, Sam's red-cheeked face in the cold, his eyes two bright dots, my arms able to lift more because he was there, too, digging with such determination, the dirty snow flying off the shovel, his parka a bright, familiar blur. I remember walking late at night to the CVS to buy orange juice, waffles, toothpaste, paper towels. And condoms. We were ritualistic about standing together before the condom display and admiring our choices: Lubricated, Ribbed, Ultrathin, Enhanced Pleasure, Pleasure Mesh, Kling Tite, Magnum, NaturaLamb.

The rule was we tried a new variety each shopping trip. The joke was we were running through condoms pretty damn quick.

I remember his apartment, three floors up, where he lived as if with his deceased wife: The address book and the recipe box still bore entries in her formal handwriting. Her black strap shoes tumbled from the bedroom closet. A snapshot of her heart-shaped face stuck to the bedroom mirror. In that apartment, when I sat at his round kitchen table, grading student papers, searching for promise and error, hearing the faint clack of Sam at his computer, two rooms away, writing code, I felt peaceful, in a domestic sort of way.

That first year, we don't talk much about the future. I want to settle down and have a child or two, and Sam simply says he is not opposed to the idea. I do not press. I dust the apartment and clean out a closet for my own use.

Fast forward to the end of our second summer. Sam is spending a lot of time in the bathroom, looking at his hair in the mirror over the sink. "Does it look thinner to you?" he asks.

I cannot see any change. His hair is as thick and black as it has ever been.

"Okay," Sam mutters. "I guess you're right." He leaves the bathroom, only to run his hand again through his locks. "Feel it," he demands. "Tell me my hair isn't thinning."

"Your hair isn't thinning," I say for the hundredth time that day.

"Something is happening," Sam complains. "Something is wrong."

I too feel something is wrong. Is he falling out of love with me? Is there someone else? When we are together now, Sam is often distracted and preoccupied. He is spending more and more time at the lab, often not coming back to the apartment until midnight. He rarely calls anymore until I leave three, four messages on his answering machine.

"I'm taking off for Chicago," Sam finally informs me. "To look into some business my father left."

"When will you be back?"

"Five days—a week."

Ten days go by and still I do not hear from him. "Maybe he's afraid of a serious commitment," Christine says. She stands in her studio, positioning a green glass bowl on top of a cigar box.

"Maybe I'm not the One." I sit on a foldout lawn chair, its weave frayed. "Maybe he's not the One. Maybe there is no such thing as the One."

Christine nods. "Look at Charlie and me. Nine years and still we don't know if we want to be together."

"Yeah, but—" Our friendship is partly based on my willingness to tolerate Christine's eccentricities and her willingness to listen to me. Out loud, I run through a list of what Sam considers my flaws. Prone to staring out windows and forgetting to turn off the stove. Solves simple arithmetic problems on her fingers. Has an uncertain income source.

My true flaw, I tell Christine, lies in letting other people decide things for me. Why should Sam be the only one to set the pace in our relationship? I remember Theo, the one before Sam, and Jerome, my college boyfriend. I allowed both men to drift away, no questions asked, no difficult good-byes required. This time will be different. I want to know what is wrong.

Which is why I find myself at Sam's door one afternoon in October 1991. I ring his bell and in the several minutes I wait for his cloppety-clop-clop down the stairs, I think of turning around.

With a little effort, Sam dislodges his warped, stuck door. "Hi," he says.

"Hi," I say.

"I've been meaning to call. Sorry."

I have never seen him as he is now: rumpled clothing and scraggly beard. "What's going on?" I say, in my best put-upon voice. "Where have you been?"

He motions me upstairs. The kitchen table is strewn with opened bills, newspapers, an eyeglass case, a thick bunch of keys, a vase with wilting iris and bachelor buttons—Sam's particular disarray, and for a moment I am calmed by just looking at his familiar objects.

Sam walks over to the sink with quick, agitated steps, not at all the easy lope I've known. "Glass of water?" He turns on the faucet. There is no cabinet under the sink, which makes the pipes too starkly visible. He hands me a tumbler of clear city water.

"Cancer," he says. "I have cancer."

I think I haven't heard right. I make him say it again.

"I might pull through it okay," he continues, too quickly. "I didn't want to worry you until I was sure. But if it hasn't metastasized, I have a pretty good chance."

A cold lozenge of fear lodges in my chest.

"Prostate cancer," Sam says in a faint voice I can barely hear, from far away, far across the room, "is slow moving. I'm lucky to have found it."

His new darting steps carry him into the side pantry, where I hear him rustling among the paper bags and old soup cans. I am alone in that spare kitchen with my shock and terror. *He's going to die* is the first thought that goes through my head. He's going to become old and ill and never come out of the hospital, just like the father of a friend from high school.

Sam returns from the pantry. Oddly enough, I am expecting him to bring me something, a treat. But he is empty handed. His eyes are a beseeching storm cloud. "I'm going to need you," he says. "To be there for me. As a friend."

And then the cold lozenge moves down to my belly, dissolving, and I feel my throat open. "A friend?" I say. "As in only a friend?" I feel angry to be rivaled by a disease.

"A friend for now." Sam speaks gently. This earnest approach, so unlike the ironic witticisms of the old Sam, shakes me almost as much as his news.

"What kind of a friend?" I ask. "A be-there-all-the-time friend or a well-wisher friend or a friend you sometimes sleep with or what?"

"Look," Sam says. "I can't promise you a future, not yet anyway, and you are free to see whom you like, but I'm going to need you."

I am pacing his small kitchen, quickly, as if to catch a train. "How do you feel?" I ask.

"Not sick," he boasts. "Far from it. I am strong and ready to fight this thing."

And then he is talking, talking at a rapid clip I can barely follow, telling me about the internist who felt an enlarged prostate gland in the digital rectal exam. Because the gland was soft as it should be and not hard as a cancer-ridden gland is typically, and because Sam is young, the doctor told Sam not to worry.

"Of course, I worried. Naturally, I did not trust him," Sam says, his eyes narrowed in anger. "Not after what I saw with my wife."

I nod. I know about the nine-inch needle and the nurse who did not hear her cries.

"Right away when I got back to Boston," Sam continues, "I had my friend Norm over at Children's set me up with a urologist." He pours another glass of water. "Gary Kearny. He has a reputation as a Finder. He ran a PSA test and it came back at 6.2."

I have no idea that 6.2 is a dangerously high marker for a 43-year-old man. I do not know that the PSA is a new and controversial blood test, that prostate cancer is still very much perceived as a geriatric disease, with Sam as a perplexing case.

"So," I say, searching for the right thing to say. Sam is ablaze now with anger and purpose. I see the bone in his elbow and the fragile way he holds himself.

"So," he continues. "We did a biopsy. It came back positive."

"And so," I stammer back. "So, what are you going to do?"

Sam gesticulates right and left. He is consulting with specialists and conducting his own research. "The data is fragmentary," he says. "Survival results merely anecdotal." What he should do is not at all clear.

I look at him that late afternoon, the maple outside his window fiery red, the light thin and burnished, the air crisp, invigorating. This time I see neither a bearded gourmet nor a wizard mathematician, not even a loose-limbed lover, but a man with an honest appeal. Mitchell said Sam had ontological depth. Now, Being itself is taking on a dark, shivery tinge. ✦

2

INVISIBLE BEAMS

The Community calls a meeting, at Miranda's house. I sit on the brown couch. I cup my hand around herbal tea in a ceramic mug. Instead of the boisterous party where Sam and I met nearly two years ago, the room is strained with silence. Miranda rearranges the little bowls of banana chips and peanuts that nobody's touched. I keep thinking about how it's warmer here on the seventh floor of Miranda's rent-controlled apartment building, with the steam radiator coughing up dry heat, than it is in my drafty Victorian. I feel my bones thaw.

"I talked with Sam this morning," says Willy.

I haven't talked to Sam for three weeks, since he announced his illness. We agreed it was best we stop seeing one another. And now I feel envious that Willy, who is Sam's best male friend in Boston, is in close contact.

"Without the Community," Sam has told me, "I could not have gotten through Andrea's illness." And so, because I promised Sam, and because I admire the idea of the Community—group support and solidarity as a solution to the isolation of the individual—and because the Community called me to this meeting, I am here. But I don't know what to say to Sam's friends. Am I an old girlfriend? A friend?

"When I talked with him this morning," Willy repeats, "he was leaning toward a decision. Radiation."

"Why not surgery?" Miranda asks. "Isn't that more sure?"

Willy shrugs. "You know Sam. He's got it all figured out. Can't tell him what to do. I'm sure he'll fill us in. Whatever he decides, we have to support that path."

Willy teaches sociology. Curly hair, beat-up tennis shoes, braided-leather wristband—he looks the part of a perpetual undergraduate.

Then Sam walks in, wearing his olive-green raincoat, a black book bag slung over his shoulder. He's wearing dark glasses. He looks like a hunted man. Everyone stands up with strange formality. No jokes or handshakes from everyone's witty friend Sam.

He sits directly across from me in Miranda's best Windsor chair. He sits very still: knees together, feet resting on the bottom rung. I am not accustomed to this much physical distance between us. I want to be back at his round kitchen table, sitting on his lap.

Sam speaks slowly. He does not remove his shades. What he does is to very deliberately remove a six-inch stack of stapled together, xeroxed papers. These he holds up: Exhibit A. "I've read the studies," he announces. "Terrance and I have been scouring the Harvard Med School building," he boasts, "where the professional journals are kept."

I look quizzically at Miranda, who is sitting beside me on the couch. "Terrance," she stage-whispers, "is our contact man in the medical establishment. Oncology Research Senior Staff."

"I've read every word," Sam goes on. "Guess what? There's no comparison of surgery with external beam radiation. No evidence that surgery will give me a better chance at survival."

"But cutting out the gland—" Miranda begins.

"I'm not letting those surgeons cut me up," he says

"What do the doctors say?" asks Willy.

Sam puts down the stack of papers. "Which one?" He folds his arms across his chest.

"All of them!" from Miranda.

"I spoke to three arrogant surgeons," Sam says. "None of them cared the slightest about complications. Hell, it's not their body."

He glances at me now, and I am surprised to feel my face momentarily warm.

"Then the fourth surgeon, a mensch, who I liked—Lenny Zinman up at the Leahy—had the intelligence not to treat me like a geriatric case. He advised against surgery."

"Advised *against?*" I am confused. Like Miranda, I'm not sure why Sam doesn't want to get the gland out once and for all.

"Yup," says Sam. "Zinman thinks the cancer is already outside the capsule. He told me to think seriously about quality of life."

"Quality of life, is that a reflection of the national GNP?" jokes Willy.

Sam doesn't hear the joke. "Impotence and incontinence," he says. "In my book, that's serious stuff."

I have never heard people speak at such length about the body's failures. In my family, you did not get ill. You got sick. You vomited and Mom put an old soup pot by the bed. You slept. You ate dry toast. You drank tea with honey and lemon. You got to watch daytime TV. The dog kept vigil on your bed. The noisy household swirled around your room and you were not in it. You slept some more.

You went to the doctor if you broke your leg or arm. That was the worst we could imagine—a limb in a white plaster cast.

Sam is not sick. No part of his body is broken. I have trouble understanding that Sam is *ill*. Sam could die. Is this why I am numb and frozen in this warm room? As for quality of life, I've always defined it as having to do with love, truth, beauty. Impotence? I can barely pronounce the word.

Sam is talking in his new slow voice. "So this fourth surgeon," he says, "referred me to Dr. Shipley, radiation oncologist. Dry Yankee humor. An ironist and a statistician. I liked him."

He likes him enough to sign up with his program. The radiation treatments will begin at the end of the month. They will last for eight weeks. Daily treatment sessions Monday through Friday, with weekends off.

"Isn't surgery more sure?" asks Miranda, not yet convinced.

"Of course, with radiation, you don't know whether you're cured," says Sam, "but I can live with that uncertainty as long as the PSA doesn't rise after treatment."

Miranda nods. "Sounds like you've made your decision." She pulls out a large appointment book from her brightly woven bag. "Why don't we each sign up for one day of the week to go to the hospital with Sam?"

I sign up for Fridays.

In truth, a person does not really need assistance for radiation treatment. Sam is capable of driving himself to treatment. But

Sam humored us. He humored me. The first Friday, Sam turns to me, strapped into the passenger seat of my Datsun hatchback, and says, matter of factly, "I've banked sperm, you know."

I did not know. Sam explains that as a result of the radiation, he will probably be sterile. The high energy beams will be aimed at the prostate gland, the part of the male reproductive system that secretes semen. High beam radiation kills the production of viable sperm.

Instead of answering, I give my attention to the traffic on the Salt and Pepper Bridge. I am thirty-four years old, I think. I am more or less single. I am having coffee tomorrow with a man I met at a poetry reading. I am driving my friend Sam to Oncology at Massachusetts General Hospital, and a white Dodge is coming up fast in my rearview mirror.

"I went three times to a sperm bank," Sam says. This memory seems to amuse him, for he throws back his head and laughs. "I filled twenty-two vials. Good, vintage sperm. More than enough for one child."

My chest rises and falls with relief. The bad news: Sam will be sterile. The good news: Now I know for sure he wants one.

In the waiting room, I think about fathers. Sam inherited this disease from his father. Sam hates his father. Hates the belt with which his father spanked him, hates his father's little moustache, hates his father's taunts: "You'll never amount to anything!" This from a man who was a community leader, a charismatic Zionist, a celebrated ophthalmologist. Sam, now, undressed, naked under a silver machine, black magic marker drawn on his groin as target lines for the radiation's charge. Sam, now, trusting to the invisible. High beams will burn out his shame. Shame on Sam the invisible son. Shame on Sam in trouble.

Invisible too, not even a glimmer yet, is Sam's future son. For Sam hopes to pass along only the smart genes, the funny genes, the genes for hitting balls and loving cars and tools, the genes for solving mathematical equations, but not the genes for aberrant prostate cells.

I see the fear now on Sam's face when he turns the corner from the treatment room. I see the quiet way he folds into himself on the ride home. He is heavy-lidded with fatigue. He pecks me good-bye on my cheek. A sweet bird peck.

When I pull up in front of my own house and turn off the ignition key, darkness has already fallen. I am afraid of being abandoned. I *am* abandoned.

During these forty days of radiation, my old friend Jerome arrives by Greyhound bus from Arizona, where he has been at a writer's colony. In one hand, Jerome swings a lumpy duffel bag and in the other, he carries a portable Olivetti typewriter. Since I have seen him last, Jerome has acquired a leather jacket and a new saunter in his walk.

I've known Jerome since college, in a time before personal computers and AIDS. Jerome has a habit of dropping in on me every couple of years. He is not what you call a suitable man for a relatively decent young woman like myself, a late bloomer in love. But I have a weakness for Jerome. With Sam sick and self-absorbed, my weakness for Jerome turns into a real need. I turn to Jerome the way I would later turn to family, friends, and therapists: for solace.

"You're looking great, just terrific," he says to me at the bus station. I wear my tightest jeans, a scoop-neck blouse.

Back at my place, we hop onto my futon. There is one thing that Jerome and I do best, and we lose no time in preliminaries. He is on top of me, inside me, pumping and pumping, and I am holding on to his broad back for dear life, my hips moving to a rising arc of desire. He smells faintly of nicotine and strongly of pheromone musk. We withhold and postpone, we receive and relinquish, we prolong the act until we can contain ourselves no longer—his explosion follows mine. He rolls off me and we lie side by side, breathing heavily, like two winded athletes. This is my carnal baseline, the sexuality with which I came of age, and I mention it here to demonstrate how far I will come—pun intended—in my erotic life with Sam and Sam's illness.

Afterward, lying in bed, Jerome and I talk. "Wow, you're a professor now," Jerome says.

I tell him about my students, my course plans, and my paycheck. Then he changes the subject.

"Any men?" my lover asks, trying to sound casual. "Any new guys?"

"There's one," I say. "He's a pack rat." I begin to describe for Jerome Sam's floor-to-ceiling newspaper piles, the thick dust layering his windowsills, his deceased wife's belongings—but then I stop. I don't tell Jerome about the birthday candles Sam produced, like a magician, from his shirt pocket at the restaurant where we dined when I turned 33, or that Sam laughs on the inhale, a plaintive sound, or the times I've taken pleasure from just being in the room and listening to Sam's voice—commanding, argumentative, solid—when he speaks on the telephone, for hours, to his broker, lawyer, mother.

"He's pretty nice" is all I say. I pull my arm out from under Jerome's. "And he has cancer."

Jerome sets up his Olivetti on my maple desk and claims a corner for his duffel bag's sprawling contents: dog-eared copies of Yeats, Roethke, and Rilke. "I'll practice the typewriter while you're out teaching," he drawls.

It seems there is an extra ingredient in Jerome's semen that makes me want more and more. Our nightly gymnastics possess me. As the weeks pass, the deeper he gets inside me, the less I am able to think clearly about the fact that I'm not getting enough sleep; I am fudging my lectures; I am paying for all the groceries. But I don't want Jerome to leave. What it comes down to is this: Sam could be dying and just now, Jerome makes me feel alive.

And still I call Sam. We are friends; I care; I hope; I know his number by heart. "Let me take you out for coffee," I say. "To celebrate the end of radiation."

At the café, I realize how bedraggled I've become. My hair and clothes need washing and my skin is splotchy, tinted with gray.

But Sam doesn't notice. "I'm feeling optimistic," he says. He is thin from the radiation. Thin, but smiling. "My PSA came back at 1.6. That's nearly undetectable. Dr. Shipley says I have every reason for guarded optimism."

We order a slice of hazelnut chocolate cake layered with fresh raspberries.

"I've been an excellent patient," he says. "I'm proud of the way

I handled my own case. Not everyone could, you know." He licks the frosting off his fork.

I nod. *He's going to be all right* is what I hear.

"As for potency," he says, looking me in the eye, "I don't know if I still have it."

I don't know how to respond to this. I have all the potency I want with Jerome. I'm not sure what I want with Sam, but I do know that looking across the table at his familiar bearded face makes me want to sing.

"I can smell him on you," barks Jerome when I get home. "Is his dick bigger than mine?"

"Oh, please," I say. "I did not have sex with him. We just talked."

Jerome mocks my pout. "We just talked. We just talked."

"Will you stop? He's a friend, all right? You seem to forget he's been sick."

Then I spot the half-empty Jim Beam bottle on my desk.

"I thought you weren't drinking," I say.

"I'm *not* drinking." He tips his glass—an old jelly jar—in my direction and grins like a weasel. "This is a special occasion." He lights a cigarette and shakes out the match one, two, three times.

"This is a no-smoking house," I say, even though he's been smoking in my room for weeks.

"I don't care," he snaps. "But I do care about us. And it appears you do not."

"I like us okay. When did I say I didn't like us?"

"You want to get married, you say, but what you don't realize is that you are no more the marrying type than I am," he accuses.

"You are a wanderer, like me. You don't want to cook and keep house for some man. Admit it, will you?"

I open my mouth to tell him that maybe he's a teeny bit correct, although it's more complicated than he's making it to be. The words never come out because I see, with slow-motion clarity, Jerome pick up my fat red Webster's, his hardball pitch, and the unfurling pages coming flying at me. Paralyzed, stunned—*so this is what it's like to be hit by a man*—I feel the breath knocked out of me. From far inside, my breastbone aches. I am stung, smarting, hurt. The room is shockingly still.

"I guess," he says, biting his words, "I better be going. I seem to have lost control of the situation."

I do not meet his eye. I do not let him see my tears. "Yeah," I say. "You better clear out your stuff right now." And then I sit silently on the foul-smelling bed while Jerome shoves his shirts and razor into the duffel bag. He and I have crossed a line together and now, in our final intimacy, something between us has irrevocably broken.

After Jerome leaves, I come down with a terrible case of the flu. I stay at my mother's house. I sleep in my childhood room; the room that was once painted pink and hung with pink Marimekko curtains. I put on a faded flannel nightgown and lie down in my twin bed and will not tell my worried mother or father what is wrong. I doze and wake in a fever's chill, the phone ringing downstairs, and hear my mother's courteous voice telling Sam I cannot come to the phone just now.

I sleep for a long time. In my dream I am nine years old again.

Summertime, when fat honeybees hover around my mother's garden and a woodpecker hammers his persistent tune up high on the towering oak. I sit outside in my shorts, drinking Kool-Aid and turning the crisp pages of a Nancy Drew book. I practice cartwheels on the front lawn. Cartwheels! When I cartwheel, I know exactly where on the damp grass to place each palm and just how high to kick my legs. In my dream I fly across the lawn in a wide, effortless arc, as again and again I turn upside down and right side up.

And then Sam is better. And then I am well.

Our first post-radiation date happens to fall on Father's Day. Will you understand how I fell for Sam if I tell you that my father and I live only twelve actual miles from each another, but that the day Sam and I officially got back together I was feeling a lifelong paternal distance? A card, a too-polite phone call . . . as a child, I heard my father as a faint buzz from the basement where he worked the power saw, building the family bookcases, shelves, bunk beds. If ever I climbed to his attic study, I'd hear the low murmur that meant he was talking numbers to himself. "Unlike life, math problems have a solution," he would say on our way down to the supper table. There, my mother wielded her power with a fierce ladle while my younger sister and brother kicked each other's shins. My seat was beside my mother, farthest from my father. The problem: He and I, the quiet ones, were lost to one another in the family hubbub.

Too easy an equation, you may say. Emotionally distant father equals daughter who falls for a man who may leave her for illness. But are not most explanations easy for the mysterious and often circumstantial ways we fall in love? Sam is certainly an antidote to Jerome. I am attracted to Sam's stability and old-fashioned values. To his moderate drinking habits and fiscal responsibility. To his concern for others than himself.

At any rate, when Sam comes to pick me up, I am sitting at a vanity table, putting on mauve lipstick. I hear him opening the downstairs lock with the key I once gave him. I hear my heart thump in my chest and I hear his bounding step on the stair, then his boisterous "Hello there! Don't you look divine!"

He is wearing an orange Gap pocket tee. He smells of milled soap and musty car upholstery. We do not kiss, but he grazes my arm shyly, in greeting.

We go out to a hip-hop concert, in Roxbury. All that sheer physical energy on stage, even the Elma Lewis dance class kids, *especially* the testosterone-tanked teenaged kids with their Raggedy Ann limbs and muscles shining bright, brings Sam and me up to a buzzing place where PSAs stay low and therefore we live happily ever after.

After the concert, we sit across from one another in a brightly lit retro diner, and down draft beers from tall glasses.

"I know I'm kind of a risk," he begins. He goes on about cure rates and testing plans. But I am not really listening. I am looking into Sam's face—strong-featured, animated, now, by the new familiarity of us in this noisy downtown night—and I just cannot believe in disease. When I look into the lines and crevices of his tawny skin and feel the welling up inside me, I believe, or I have to believe, that he is better and that my love will keep him well. Did I say that he is better? That we are better, lighter, more attractive, and in finer sync to the other's cues.

"I'd like to see," he says, starting in on a mound of garlicky mashed potatoes, "how far it goes with us this time."

We are visible to one another in a way we have not been before. I feel *seen*. I feel excited. I feel full of possibility. And maybe, just maybe, I think, tipping back my glass, the cold beer tickling the back of my throat, the furious wheels of denial gaining momentum from the fact that he was always asymptomatic, maybe the whole ordeal was nothing but a medical error. ✦

3

BRIDAL LACE

My sister always dreamed of herself as Cinderella meeting her Prince at the ball and then marrying him in the castle. In the plays I wrote as a child, she was the Princess and wore a silver sheath of a flapper dress that somehow found its way into our dress-up box. With her golden hair billowing down to her waist and supporting a rhinestone tiara, her habit of sighing heavily as she sat down on an armchair, and her regal posture as she crossed the room, she played the part convincingly. My best friend, Tokiko, was the Prince, required to wear khakis and a tie and to walk around with my sister, the Princess, on her arm.

I played the witch. I dressed in black; I knew secret spells; I perfected my cackle. Already, I was cynical, reserving myself for pursuits more interesting than romantic love. Or was it simply that with my frizzy brown hair and athletic frame I could not compete with my sister's golden locks and willowy shape?

I was a late bloomer, and I never much contemplated marriage until my midtwenties. Boys I was crazy about, and adventures of every kind, but marriage seemed a bland, far-off country. My parents didn't pressure me. My friends were waitressing and trying to be dancers or going to graduate school. At some point, I think when I was in graduate school myself, in Salt Lake City, where custom dictated that a girl be engaged by high school graduation and married two years later, when her fiancé returned from his mission, I began to warm to the idea of a more permanent commitment to a man. I was tired of saying good-bye to boyfriends. I read Jane Austen, Jean Rhys, William Wordsworth, Wallace Stevens. These books had the effect of making me more serious about my life. Choices had consequences, I learned from my authors, and a person could make his or her own meaning of things. I owned one plate, two forks, three bowls; the day I found myself preoccupied with arranging these paltry items in the cupboard just so was the day I decided I wanted to get married. For I suddenly saw the course my solitary life was heading: I was becoming a weird, introverted person, a recluse unable to tolerate a bowl out of place. I could see myself in ten years as a fussy and timid woman. In company, I'd talk too much or too little. Besides, I wanted a child.

When I move back to Boston at the ripe old age of 30, it is with the express intention of finding someone to marry. I am not so choosy. I want a reasonable man with whom I can have a family and continue to write. He should be attractive and smart enough. He cannot be a substance abuser. And, oh yes, he should love me.

Sam fits the bill. He is funny and unusual. Plus, he is Jewish. This second time we get together after he is well, after our date at the hip-hop concert, our feelings quickly deepen and grow. Cancer-free Sam wants to forge ahead with his life, with our life. "I could get used to this," he says to me. By now, I am used to his understatement. And his passion: "I feel like my whole life has led me to you," he confesses. "Ladylove," he calls me. "*My* ladylove."

The twenty-minute commute between our apartments becomes an unbearable distance. When Sam stays at my place, he invariably forgets his contact lens solution; at two in the morning we must bid each other a very reluctant good-bye. And Larry and Christine have moved on, a new generation of housemates moved in. I'm living with strangers who want to haggle over whose turn it is to buy a roll of toilet paper! Sam and I decide to live together, as per the custom in our circle. I refuse to move in to his place, to the apartment he shared with his wife, the third-floor walkup beside the train tracks he's hated for years. Soon we are spending our free time together looking at real estate.

Over the phone one Sunday in March, Sam explains that he's just made a deposit on a house, apologizing for making the decision without me but explaining that a line of renters were waiting to snap it up. When I see the place, a whole house in West Cambridge, a charming old workers' cottage with pine floorboards, wainscoting, and a circular stair, I feel a new kind of trust for this man. To think that I was ready to rent the apartment with a bedroom window looking out on a brick wall! But Sam held out for the lucky find. And then he knew when to act. I can rely on his real-world skills. He is my lucky find.

The April evening we move in there is a freak snowstorm, and then the next day the temperature rises to sixty degrees and everything melts, the sun a blessing. I poke around in the yard, the forsythia bush a bright yellow spot. Sam comes outside, stands behind me. "Lucky in real estate," he says. "Lucky in love, too?"

I lean back, rest my head on his chest. "Doesn't seem like too much to ask."

"Come in," he says. "Help me unpack the kitchen."

"The way you say that," I tease, "is so seductive."

Six large cartons sit in the middle of the kitchen, their tops already split open with an Exacto knife. The kitchen is large and dark, with brick red linoleum and wood veneer cabinets. From the first carton, Sam and I pull newspaper bundles: juice glasses, wine glasses, Cuisinart, plates. Serving bowls, cereal bowls, green pitcher, spoons.

We unwrap each bundle as if it's a gift. When we pull away our hands, we find them stained with black ink.

"All this stuff," I say.

"My dowry," jokes Sam.

"The end of my gypsy days." Since moving to Boston from Utah, I've acquired a few more dishes, a space heater, and a fourteen-inch television set. Living in a communal house, I hadn't needed to actually *buy* things. Only now does my austerity strike me as odd.

I unpack a pewter pitcher, still in its original box, never used. "This looks like a wedding present."

"We'll get our own things," he says. "Little by little."

Sam owns a full set of flatware, a bed with a headboard, an omelet pan. That he is so heavily weighted in the material world comforts me. His things ground me. He's held onto a vacuum cleaner for fifteen years, a toaster oven for ten. He believes in buying top quality and then taking good care. If he's that attached to a vacuum cleaner, I think, he must really stick to a woman. He will not discard me; he will take good care.

I don't like to eat off the same plate as Andrea did, but I don't tell him because I'm afraid he'll be offended. All the same, I don't like him assuming I can just pick up where Andrea left off.

"What about this?" I say in our new kitchen. I hold up a heavy brown bowl that's covered with a heavy brown lid. There are five more exactly like it. "What are these?"

"Onion soup bowls."

"But there's another whole set of perfectly good soup bowls!" I point to the white earthenware stack on the counter. "When was the last time you made onion soup?"

"I used those bowls in 1979 when Benni Efrat and his then-wife came to dinner. Believe me, it was good soup."

"You've been holding on to these for fifteen years?"

Sam looks up at the dropped ceiling. "I think I used them again in 1982, when Hayward Alker and Ann Tickner came to dinner. That was before Andrea got sick."

Suddenly I hate these bowls. I hate brown with tan streaks. These bowls shout a warning message: how difficult it is for Sam to let go of the past and how afraid he is of change. I'm horrified he even took the time to pack them.

"We don't have room," I say. I gesture to the boxes in the middle of the floor and then the bank of cabinets. "We have to get all this stuff put away. And there's just not room for onion soup. All that cheese is bad for you."

He's so rooted in the past; whereas I'm thinking about keeping his arteries clear of fat so he lives a long time, and about having a child, who will need room in the cabinets for sippy cups, and about my age, thirty-six, almost thirty-seven, tick tick tick. I find it bewildering, sometimes, how one minute Sam and I are in the garden all lovey dovey and the next we're bickering about domestic details.

I am not used to experiencing such a range of emotions with one person. Most people know me as levelheaded and pleasant. In grade school, I was the one the teacher left in charge if she was called away to a phone call. She could count on me to be responsible. From there, it was easy to see myself as a good girl. Easy for the adults around me, too. Less known was the sixteen-year-old girl who slipped out of the house at night to go skinny dipping in Crystal Lake with her boyfriend, or the twenty-year-old young woman buying bags of Acapulco Gold, or the young adult with contradictory desires: Writing or children? Marriage or freedom? Princess or witch?

Sam is one of the few people I know with whom I can be angry, ambitious, and selfish, as well as kind, generous, and loving. You wouldn't think this to be an endorsement for true love, but in my case, I feel my whole self embraced.

Another thing I'm learning from Sam is how to come right out and say what's on my mind. I admire his frankness. My style is to be circular, suggestive, covert. For example, very casually, pouring the morning coffee, I remark: "I spoke to my mother the other day and she asked me if we were going to get married."

"So you want to get married!" he retorts.

"Well, I'm thinking about it. I mean, we're not getting any younger. If we want to have kids . . ."

"You have my love. You have my commitment," he booms. "I've even agreed to have a child. What more do you want?"

"To be an honest woman," I tease.

"The Talmud says . . ."

"You and your Talmud." I throw up my hands in exasperation. I walk to the hall, gather my keys, my purse, and my briefcase. I know what he's going to say. The Talmud says there are three ways of marrying a woman. By sexual intercourse, by money, and by contract in an official ceremony. Sam claims that by writing the deposit check for our house he has done two out of the three.

And then it's fall, and every day when I drive to work on Storrow Drive I pass maples and oaks swaying with brilliant color along the Charles River. I'm teaching a creative writing class now, too, along with my usual steady diet of freshman composition. I love my students, their imagination and enthusiasm, their budding stories. I love the old brick building where my office is housed and my large, windowed office, borrowed from a professor on leave, and my friend Irene right next door with whom, between student visitors, I have whispered conversations in the hallway.

On days when I do not teach, I sit in my sloped-ceiling office at home and read and write. I am placing poems in magazines. I am learning to write stories. I buy a pretty notebook at Pier 1 and fill it with a hurried scrawl, only to discover that I have written a novel, almost unintentionally, and it's pretty good.

It's late 1994, and the Internet is about to break big time. Sam and his team fly back and forth to Washington, D.C., to meet with Al Gore's chief techies. They have designed a software system for White House publications over the Internet. They now envision hundreds of government workers able to have online meetings. Technology is to revive participatory democracy, if not the power of the common worker. Sam is at the lab, working until nine or ten at night most weekdays. He comes home elated, charged. I stumble downstairs from my office and we meet in the kitchen. We talk about our day, in casual detail, in the way of good friends. I make pasta with diced garlic and olive oil; Sam opens a can of tuna, uncorks a bottle of wine.

We leave the dirty dishes in the sink. We fall into bed, exhausted, and sleep all night nestled like spoons.

It's fall, and Sam is due for another semi-annual PSA test. We can never be sure that the radiation zapped every last cancerous cell. His last score, at 2.2, is optimistically low. As long as the test remains low, we can be optimistic that the cancer is gone. The test will tell whether and how fast the disease is growing. Sam must call his primary care physician to request a form that authorizes and instructs the medical lab, pick up that form during regular office hours, walk down the hall to have his blood drawn, and then, the following week, call the doctor back for results. You'd think this would be rather cut-and-dried for someone who manages intercontinental travel with ease. Instead, Sam delays, delays, delays. And I, to my surprise, have changed into a nagging kind of girlfriend. "Have you called the doctor yet?" I ask.

"I've got to finish this project first," he says. "It'll interfere with my concentration."

"Your health is more important," I say.

"It's just a formality," he says. "Don't worry. I'm cured."

"Sam, when are you going to call?"

"What's the rush?" he says. "Even if it looks like I'm in trouble, they're not going to do anything."

"Sam, when are you going to call? I want you to call *today!*"

Finally, he calls, he goes in. During this week, gloom settles into each crevice and floorboard of the house. Our spiral stair suddenly feels narrow and steep; the pine floor, I notice, is mercilessly scuffed. My body is a heavy weight I must carry. Sam complains that the coffee is weak, the bread stale. A vein in his forehead throbs uncontrollably.

"I want you to know how to change a tire," says Sam.

"Change a tire?"

"For when I'm gone. I'm not going to be here forever, you know. It's time you learned how to do these things for yourself."

I point out that number one, I lived many years by myself without changing a tire; two, I have a lifetime membership to AAA; and three, he's not checking out any time soon.

In the middle of that dead dark night, the city eerily quiet, he wakes me up. "You're going to hire a nurse," he says. "I don't want you sacrificing your life for me if I get sick."

"Sam, I'm asleep. And you are not sick."

But he is awake with fears and plans. "I'm telling you, it gets very overwhelming. You have no idea how stressful it gets. When Andrea was in the hospital . . ."

So this is about Andrea, I think. Post-traumatic stress disorder rears its ugly head in the face of PSA anxiety. Because no one should have to go through what Sam went through with his first wife, least of all me, I am awake now, listening to Sam talk. He told no one at the lab about her illness, just grit his teeth and kept on working. He hunted for ground-floor apartments when she became too weak to climb stairs. His parents never came to visit when she was sick, not once; they were too busy, and when they finally flew east for the funeral, his mother treated the trip as a shopping spree.

I listen and listen until *I* begin to feel sick. "Sam," I finally say. I reach over for his hand. "This is all just so, so bad. I'm so sorry."

His hand is restless, resistant inside mine. He's thrashing, still in the throes of it.

"I'm just trying to prepare you," he says. "You should know these things."

"It's not going to happen to you," I say. "Let's not jump to conclusions, okay? It's only a routine test."

But his mood is contagious, and the next day I have caught it, like a rare flu to which cancer survivors and their partners are susceptible. I, too, begin to rehearse his death. I cannot imagine life without him. His absence feels enormous. I feel myself becoming utterly undone, and when Sam comes home that evening my eyes are swollen from crying.

Our moods swing, pendulum fashion. Two days later, the call comes. The doctor calls Sam at work, and Sam relays the news to me. I'm at my office, in conference with a student. Sam's PSA is stable, at 2.4.

"Oh, Sam," I say. "That's great news." I want to be at home, surrounded by his arms. I want him to be uncorking a bottle of champagne and then drinking in the bubbly. I replace the receiver in its cradle. *Thank you, thank you.*

I turn back to the basketball player in my office who is pleading his grade.

January semester break, Sam takes me to Palm Springs to visit his 79-year-old mother, Mildred. I have met her twice before, briefly, under hurried circumstances, and now we are to spend five days under the same roof.

Sam parks in front of a long stucco house with an attached garage and flowering cacti lining the drive. Sam goes into the house first, I follow, both of us carrying our bags and dressed too warmly for this tropical climate, and there is Mildred. Wearing crisply pressed white slacks, a white blouse striped with gold, hair pouffed in metallic blond, she stands expectant, poised.

She walks up to Sam, so that her chin is level with his shoulders. "You're late. I was worried sick. And now you're here." Her voice is gravelly, low.

"Mom," he says. "What could I do? There was a lot of traffic."

She turns away in disgust. What son of hers cannot circumvent mere traffic?

She steps away, down the marble walkway, across the white carpeted living room, to stand surrounded by delicate jade and ivory figurines, Chagall and Agam lithos, a large crystal vase filled with orange silk poppies. The light bounces off the mirrored cab-

inets and onto her pearl button earrings, which are large enough,
I later discover, to hide her hearing aid. A cut-glass chandelier
hangs over a glass dining room table. The couches are upholstered, white and pink. In the center of it all, modeling, is Mildred.
Never have I seen a woman so fiercely merged with her house.
She is staring at me, studying my expression. I can feel her ea-
gerness for me to like this house with the same force one feels a
lover's desire. My stomach turns over at such an immaculate, un-
touchable museum, not at all my style. But I feel her vulnerability.
And it *is* beautiful, in the shimmery, impressive way the lobby of
the Ritz is beautiful.

Besides, I want her to like me, perhaps as badly as she wants
me to like her house. She is a force in Sam's life, and I want her
as an ally.

"It's beautiful," I say. "What a beautiful, beautiful treasure."

This seems to be the right thing to say, for immediately she
snaps out of her trance and addresses Sam with a sharp voice,
bouncing from topic to topic. "Put your bags in the far bedroom.
Do you like my hair? I made sure to go to the beauty parlor today.
Where do you want to eat? Did you rent a car? I thought we'd
drive down 111 to Poisy Pansies in Rancho Mirage. A new place
that Joan recommended. What took you so long? Didn't you
know I'd be worried sick? Let's go. I've made a reservation. I don't
want to be late."

I sit in the back seat of the Ford Taurus. In front, Mildred is
talking, talking, talking to her son. I can make out only part of
what she's saying. Municipal bonds, home owners' insurance, eq-
uity gains. Sam is nodding, interjecting small comments. I am
tired and a bit overwhelmed by the strangeness of all this, and so
I concentrate on looking out at the road, which is dark and wide,
with gray mountain ranges looming everywhere, and palm trees

decorated with winding lights, as if it is always Christmas in Palm Springs. We cross Gene Autry Drive. Sam turns to me in the back seat. He points to a narrow road that winds up the looming mountain. Up high, I see a small compound of lights, low buildings. "That's where Bob Hope lives," he says.

We cross Frank Sinatra Drive.

"Where the hell are we?" I say, quietly enough so that his mother will not hear. "Is there a Janis Joplin Drive? Jimi Hendrix Circle?"

Sam laughs. Alas, those roads are not yet built.

At dinner—stuffed sole, baked potato—Mildred directs her attention to me. "I want you to know," she says, "that it's all good. I'm *for* you. I've never seen Sam look so happy and relaxed. And I want him *settled* before I die."

I like her frankness. It is so like Sam's. I like her smudged blue eye shadow and the miniature knickerbocker man on her key ring. I like the pointed directions she gives to the waiter: dressing on the side, an extra plate, no ice in her water, the check please. "Is that all, dear?" he asks.

Her laughter rings with the flirtatious fun of yesteryear. "Tell me what *you* would have for dessert."

It's late when we return to Mildred's house, and even later for Sam and me, who still are on East Coast Time. Mildred turns off the alarms, turns on the lights, and then disappears into a cavernous room. Sam sits down on the floor of the living room, so large it's called a great room. He loosens his shirt, removes his shoes. Then, in slow-motion exhaustion, he falls back onto the rug, his black curly hair a wreath on the carpet's plush pile.

I lie down beside him, careful not to muss my dress. I breathe in faint whiffs of Fantastik. "Let's sleep here," I say only half-jokingly. "The bedroom is so far away."

He reaches for my hand and begins to move his fingers across my palm. "Tell me about the desert," I say. "Will you protect me from rattlesnakes?"

"Oh yes," he says sleepily. "You can never be too careful about rattlesnakes. But don't worry. If anything bites, I'll have my mouth on your skin, madly sucking out the poison."

We hear his mother shriek. "No! No Sam no!"

Her voice is the one used on a dog who has soiled.

"Up! Up!" she shouts. "The oils from your hair! They'll ruin the fibers. Do you know how much it costs to do a room this size?"

We retreat to the bedroom, like dogs with tails between their legs. We fall onto the nearer of the two twin beds, pressed close. "I want to touch you everywhere," whispers Sam. "Let the bodily fluids flow. I'll be damned if I'm going to be careful of the sheets."

In the morning, Mildred is sitting at her glass-top kitchen table, hunched over the newspaper's daily crossword. Her bouffant hairstyle is covered with a net. She's wearing turquoise blue mules and her toenails are painted magenta. She looks up when I slide into the room, her eyes wet and a little gooey behind thick glasses. "The day I cannot figure this puzzle," she announces, "is the day I go over to the other side."

The rest of the visit she plies me with gifts. A Dana Buchman black velour tunic. Lizwear and loungewear. A butterfly brooch. An electric teakettle. First edition Philip Roth and Saul Bellow. Whatever I admire in her house, she tells me to take home. When I protest, she insists in such a way that to refuse would be an offense.

Early on, she and I understand the coding of our transactions. Mildred is elderly, frail, and could go at any time. Again and again she is handing me her son. Again and again I am saying yes.

43

Yes, I will stay with him. Yes, I will care for him. Yes, I know he's been sick.

July, and I turn thirty-eight. I don't want to celebrate my birthday this year. I feel old. To mark the occasion, I make an appointment with a nurse-practitioner in the OB/GYN department of my HMO.

The nurse-practitioner's name is Eleanor. She is in her fifties, but she wears an ankle-length, loose-fitting cotton jumper, sandals, dangling bead earrings. Her office is painted peach. The books on her shelf are about midwifery, breastfeeding, herbs. Her smile is eager, attentive. *You can confide in me.*

"I'm thinking about getting pregnant," I say.

The smile gets wider. She leans forward; our faces are close. She nods up and down in vigorous encouragement. *So many women are putting off babies these days,* I can almost hear her say. *Only to be full of regret.*

"My boyfriend . . ." I say. Immediately, the smile disappears.

"The man I live with," I continue, "has sort of an unusual situation. I mean, we're working with banked sperm."

Her eyebrows go up. Quickly, I explain Sam's cancer, radiation treatment, sterility—the banked and frozen sperm. "So you see," I conclude, "I will need medical assistance right from the get-go to get pregnant."

Creases appear on Eleanor's brow, as if she is having trouble assimilating the information. "Wait," she says. "Back up. You're talking about a *boy*friend."

"We plan to get married," I say. "Pretty soon."

Her eyebrows go up again. What I say is true, but in this room I feel suspect, not credible. I don't dare tell her that at my age a wedding seems almost superfluous compared to a birth.

"Well." I hear the coldness in her voice now. "I suppose we can do a basic fertility workup on you. See how you check out." She smoothes the wrinkles from her skirt. "Of course, we'll have to run tests on his sperm."

Now it is my turn to be puzzled. "Why sperm tests? You'd have to thaw some of the supply to do that, wouldn't you? There's a limited amount; Sam calls it a nonrenewable resource. I know it's kind of iffy for me to get pregnant, being thirty-eight and all, but I want to give it a try."

"Tests for *your* safety," she says. "HIV. STD."

I raise my hand, as if to push away these diseases. "No, no," I say. "He doesn't have any of that. He only has cancer."

But she is very serious about her job, advising that I can never be too sure the sperm is safe and she'd say the same to any one of her three grown daughters, not to mention the tricky coverage issues between his health insurance and mine, and really, I should consider an anonymous sperm donor, one of theirs, pretested and guaranteed to be disease-free.

When Sam gets home that evening, I say: "We have to get married."

"Who gets married anymore?"

I tell him about my experience with the nurse-practitioner. "It was so humiliating," I tell him. "They give you more respect if you're married."

"And you're going to let an old goat like her get to you?"

"Sam! You're not the one who has to go through the damn infertility treatments."

45

"I'm sorry," he says. "For what I'm making you go through."

"No, it's not that," I say. "I don't blame you for the infertility treatments. Besides, I might need them anyway at my age."

"It's just that marriage is such a convention," he says. "Such an arrangement of the state. I've been married, and I can tell you it's not all it's cracked up to be."

"But I haven't. Every one should try it, at least once."

"In my case, more than once."

"Why not? Besides, if we are lucky enough to have a kid, I don't want it going to kindergarten and having to talk about mom and her boyfriend."

"Lots of kids do," says Sam.

"Well, not mine. Not when the boyfriend is in fact the father."

He presses his lips together as if suppressing the urge to say more. Then he runs his hand through his hair and presses the play button on the answering machine, checking his messages.

On my wedding day, I dress in black leggings, boots that hug my calf, and a tawny gold silk tunic with an iridescent leaf pattern. I stand before the bathroom mirror and brush out my shoulder-length hair. I put on all my makeup; my face is tinted and smooth. I look strangely composed. In the mirror is a woman neither old nor young, with wide parted lips, dark slanted eyes. She looks surprisingly old-fashioned, like a woman in a sepia photograph from the beginning of the last century.

I hear Sam's step on the tile, see his face beside mine in the mirror. He, too, has undergone a transformation, as if calling up the spirit of his ancestors. His usually angular face has narrowed to a scholar's elongated shape. His beard is a thin line around his jowls. His eyes are bright, his lips pressed together in a half-smile. We look like a couple that stands together to face adversity. Two people able to weather diphtheria, Nazis, subversive lists, still-birth, immigration, drought—all of which our combined ancestry did, in fact, survive. Personal fulfillment, conjugal bliss . . . when did marriage become about these effervescent luxuries?

Up to sixty percent of contemporary marriages break up in the first five years. Married women have a higher incidence of depression than single women do. And yet, and yet . . . I want to try this formal commitment. What do I expect? A warm body lying beside me at night, proof that I am not entirely alone in the world. Someone to kill the creepy-crawly bugs that climb the walls in summer. A face I know well to see across the supper table. A person who will love me, bleary-eyed, at the breakfast table.

Outside, in our driveway, winter's chill is in the air, the sky whitening. We drive down Broadway and then down a cobbled side street for an eleven o'clock appointment to see Sam's shrink. Ziv.

Sam and I sit close beside one another on his therapist's futon couch. My leg touches Sam's, my heart beats in its tight cage. I tell Ziv, this man with a sardonic reserve to whom each week Sam entrusts his soul, that I wish Sam could be more, well, enthusiastic, about marrying me. "This secret civil ceremony," I accuse, "is not exactly a celebration."

"I'm not going to make a spectacle of myself again," growls Sam. "That's what weddings are."

"Well, I wouldn't know."

"What's wrong with City Hall?" he says. "The IRS doesn't mind."

I look pleadingly at Ziv. Help me out here. Be on my side. Yet, in truth, a part of me is relieved not to have to spend a year plan-

ning what kind of appetizers to serve a hundred and one guests. I
have seen too many capable women friends lose their intelligence
to swathes of bridal lace. As much as I object, Sam's unconventional, even subversive wedding has saved me for myself, and
given me a way to almost circumvent the bonds of matrimony.
Isn't marriage supposed to tie one down? Marrying at City Hall,
perhaps I can hold onto the witch's power I felt as a girl. I still
know some secret spells: I am a poet who can pore over ancient
manuscripts and decipher meaning from a few arcane words. I still
dress in black; I still cackle, if only quietly and behind my hands.
What self-respecting witch would submit to scented invitations?

Yet another, small, girlish part of me wants to be the Princess
I never was, to be pampered and indulged. I think of my sister,
who was married seven years ago in a Laura Ashley gown, under
a rose arbor, her smile dazzling a generous array of loved ones.
My sister and her husband-to-be rented a two-hundred-year-old
mansion on the grounds of a nature conservancy. A little rain fell
after the ceremony.

I could feel my sister's happiness radiating. Her happiness was
in her smile, which came easily and full, with none of the slight
grimacing tugs she exhibited before meeting Scott. Her happiness was in her movements, so fluid and lovely, as she held the
train of her gown in her hand, the new gold band catching a
flicker of sun. Her happiness was like sunlight streaming through
a window so bright my eyes hurt. No matter where I stood—by
the bar set up on the veranda, where a well-intentioned, conde-
scending friend of my mother's said, "You'll find someone, too,"
or by my sister's throng of friends, to whom I was invisible, or
even by my great-aunt Henrietta, married to her third husband,
who tsk-tsked between her teeth and hissed, "It's not a *Jewish* wedding," I could not escape the blinding glare that was my sister's
wedding day.

Obviously, I was feeling pretty desperate about men. I'd been home from Utah for six months and had just moved out of my parents' house and into the house in Jamaica Plain with Larry and Christine. I wasn't going out with anyone. I wasn't even breaking up with someone. I was just plain single.

So single, in fact, that after the wedding luncheon, when I stood at a side table, resolutely *not* contra-dancing, a family friend of my sister's brand new in-laws came over to me. She wore a silk leopard-print top, the kind that crisscrosses the bodice; white tailored slacks; and spike heels. After the wedding, she told me, she and her husband were going to spend a week at their pied-à-terre in Manhattan. This new friend and I chitchatted for a while about the wonderful weather, save that little bit of good luck rain. Finally, she leaned closer to me. Her perfect nostrils flared. "I would never have let my younger sister get married before me. I made sure I got married *first*."

I turned away to watch the knee-raising dancers struggling to keep up with the fiddler's sly tune. What she says hurts more than I'd like to admit. Here I am trying to be happy for my sister's happiness when really this entire wedding is a slap to my face. I remember hearing how my grandmother waited for three years to marry my grandfather until his older brother found a wife. My grandfather Benzion Propp was from an Orthodox home, his father a devout Jew from Lithuania. The way my grandmother told the story, it was a terrible affront to have to wait so long to marry her beloved. As I got older, I realized that she told the story to justify my grandfather's nightly visits to her on what she called "the couch in the sunroom."

But that is another tale for another time. Except that today, smarting from the leopard lady's remark, I realize the reasoning behind the old-fashioned custom of my grandmother's time: personal honor. With all the talk about self-esteem and self-image, I think honor is an underrated emotion in these contemporary times. Much as I love my sister and do not want to hurt her with these words, I cannot get around this fact: My honor was publicly wounded.

When I start thinking about honor, I realize why I hate the dress I am wearing, the dress my sister and my mother insisted I wear. It comes down to my ankles, has a lacy Peter Pan collar, and is cut from a pink-and-white floral pattern. The dress is much too sweet and girlie for me, makes me look like a sexless old maid. My sister and mother insisted I wear it because, they argued, that although my sister did not have bridesmaids in matching dresses, all the same she wanted me, as her one and only sister, to be her maid of honor, which meant standing beside her during the ceremony and reading a Wendell Berry poem, and because I was officially part of the ceremony it wouldn't look right if I didn't somehow *blend in*. Which is why my sister and mother—during the prenuptial preparations they'd suddenly become an indivisible unit—absolutely and totally vetoed the green silk dress that tugged at my hips and showed off my legs, the dress I'd bought in Macy's basement with my old friend Heidy, before she got sick with a rare and incurable cancer from which she was now dying in D.C.

"A party," I say to Sam now. Sam, my intended. Sam, the man who would never ask me to wear a dress with a Peter Pan collar and who thinks I am sexy in the green silk shift. "A party in our dining room," I say. I can see myself in a simply tailored white linen dress. A single rose in my hair. Open-toed shoes. A jazz ensemble playing edgy but upbeat improvisations. A chuppah in our driveway, which will be covered in tiny white shells for the occasion. Expensive champagne in fluted glasses. Food catered by a chef chosen by Sam. People making witty toasts that go on far too long. At least one relative making a toast in dubious taste. Mildred entertaining people decades younger than she with shocking pronouncements. My parents, made proud. My sister and brother, in support. Guests dressed in a style both premeditated and casual. Children running around and making noise. "We have to have at least that," I say.

"In May," Sam concedes. "In May, when the weather's better and my mother can travel."

Ziv turns to me. "His first marriage, you know, did not exactly end well. It's understandable that he feels some, well, some anxiety and resistance to getting married. After the trauma."

I nod. I take Sam's hand.

To Sam, Ziv bends his head and says, "There is love between you two."

It feels like a blessing.

And then we are Massachusetts Avenue–bound, where we have a twenty-minute wait for our appointment at City Hall. We duck into the 1369 Café, an old favorite. We order cappuccino and chocolate-covered biscotti. We sit at a nicked table, our knees touching in the crowded corner. A fresh-ground caffeine buzz is in the air. Herbie Hancock plays his piano over the sound system; the nose-ringed guy who works the cash register is tapping out the beat on the countertop.

"My last moments as a single woman," I sigh melodramatically.

"Want to change your mind?"

I shake my head. "I've wanted this for too long."

"Yeah," he says. "I know."

"What does a person have left at the end of life?" I say. "I want something more tangible than just all this talking and touching and fighting and making up and doing the dishes and going out to restaurants. I want a real event. Besides, I happen to love you."

"Love is not the problem," he says. "I'm just afraid of what marriage will do to us." But his eyes soften as he says this. As we walk out the door, he slides his arm around my waist, pulls me to him.

The sky has cleared, the wind died down, and the day is almost sunny as we mount the stone steps to City Hall. We find the office for the City Clerk. We hand over our blood test results, which are negative for gonorrhea and syphilis, negative for HIV, positive for love, for it is our blood we are joining today, the same blood that sang six years ago in the bustling living room where we met.

The City Clerk turns out to be a pleasant matron in a bright suit. She ushers us in to her chambers, which are lined with thick legal tomes. We are to face another and hold hands, thereby sealing our words as a legal contract.

"I apologize," she says, with a twinkle in her eye, "that the state must interfere with your personal lives."

Sam grins widely. "We won't hold it against you."

Everything is going to be okay.

As per the laws of Cambridge, Massachusetts, we pledge friendship, support, respect, and love.

"No obey!" I exclaim.

"No forsaking all others," he says merrily.

His hand in mine is a long, smooth plane, and I feel his warmth pulsing like a source of perpetual energy.

Neither one of us pledges to be there for the other in sickness and in health. The city of Cambridge does not require this assurance. Perhaps that is why it is so easy to deny the illness that still hovers over our lives, the illness I would banish with our vows. By this omission, I have not pledged to be Sam's nurse. Being a nurse is not an ambition of mine, nor is health care a talent. But I have pledged my support, which in my case means to stand by Sam should he become ill. Everything will be okay, he tells me whenever I worry about his health. I believe him, every time. Besides, thousands of people survive cancer and go on to live full lives—why shouldn't Sam and me?

What have we really pledged? What does anyone promise in marriage, that great gamble?

I have pledged to be a person named Karen, a woman with a butterfly-shaped mole on her right thigh who loves artichokes and waffles, who does not read maps well but knows certain important routes by heart. I possess patience, passion, sensitivity, forgiveness—qualities that will be sorely tested. And he has pledged to be a person named Sam, a man with shapely feet, his toes even and smooth. He loves goat cheese and peanuts; he reads maps well but does not always know his own heart. His qualities: tough-mindedness, generosity, passion, forgiveness.

Neither of us can promise to remain the person we are now. Why do we ever believe that the person we marry will stay the same?

Then, who will he be? A healthy or a sick person? Who will I be? Witch or princess, or both?

And us?

Very quietly, because the streets of our town have become lit now with a strange, yellow-gray light, we go home. Sam shucks the oysters I bought two days ago from a fisherman on Wellfleet Bay. His knife slips neatly between the two sides of the shell, which open to the delicate white flesh. I raise the hard shell, tip it into my mouth, and taste the wet, salty meat.

I pour the white wine we have chilled and I look across the table at my new husband. His eyes are two mesmerizing beams.

He reaches for my hand and I lead him up our winding stair to the bedroom, where we soon shed our clothes. Skin to skin, breathing in unison now, he slips in easily. *Husband,* I think to myself as I embrace his lean frame. *My husband.* Just now it is a new and dear word. Really, everything is so simple: an arm, an ear, a ridged spine, a thigh. We are ringed in light, this man and me. Where he goes, I go. Where I go, he goes.

We lie together a while.

And then, outside our second-story window, the storm hits full force. The sky clouds charcoal gray, turning day into sudden night. Hail the size of kidney beans pellet the ground, and the wind gusts strong enough so that the next day the sidewalk in front of our house is littered with fallen branches. ✦

BIRTH

The baby is five days late and a sonogram is ordered to view my interior. Swimming into view on the screen, scrunched in the proverbial fetal position, there he is: a perfect infant, head correctly positioned down, arms and legs floating luxuriously. My placenta is thick and nourishing. I can carry; I can hold; and of this I am proud.

I am as huge as a ship. I, who have always been tall—by sixth grade I was ashamed of being larger than the boys; by junior high I had developed a permanent slump; by adulthood I longed to be petite, frail, feminine—love being hugely pregnant. I'm blooming with possibility and prowess. To judge from the glances of approval I receive from passersby, I am doing an excellent job of continuing the species. For the first time in my life as a woman, big feels beautiful.

I who took so long and worked so hard to become pregnant—eighteen months of fertility treatments, conceiving at last with the help of a complicated in vitro procedure—do not want to give up my expectant state. Besides growing big, I love carrying a secret life. I love drinking a glass of orange juice and then, as the sugar hits his blood, feeling the baby's energetic kick. I love knowing when he sleeps, and touching my belly for his tiny foot. I sit on the couch, my feet up, and close my eyes to listen to Sarah Vaughan, my pleasure amplified by knowing that the baby, too, hears such rich harmony.

I wouldn't mind being pregnant for another month or two.

But the baby is seven days late. The baby must come out. Soon.

We're set with baby gear, baby preparations, so it feels only natural, given our extra time, to turn our attention to the family nest. All through my pregnancy we looked at real estate. The high-ceilinged mansion on Mt. Auburn Street that proved to be termite ridden; the duplex with a Zen rock garden and weirdly triangular rooms; the two-family with a hot tub on the back porch priced too high—on and on. Nothing is right for us. It's 1997, and the market is cranking up; buyers are bidding on the morning of the day a property is put up for sale.

So when our landlady Betsy calls and casually mentions that she intends to sell our very house this coming spring, although of course we could make an offer anytime—and, by the way, is the baby here yet?—Sam practically yells into the receiver: "Let's talk. Can you come over this afternoon?"

This afternoon is a hot one in early September. What with my unwieldy mass and the close, unmoving air, I move as little as possible. I lower myself into the antler chair in the living room, a tall glass of ice water in hand. Betsy and Sam sit on the couch. "It's a solid house," she is saying. "Good bones, good foundation."

"We have a good feeling here," says Sam. "We're attached to the place."

"Not many single families for sale left in Cambridge anymore," adds Betsy.

"With a yard," I say.

"A very small yard," says Sam.

"When would we have to decide?" I ask Betsy.

"No rush," she says. She glances at my ballooning belly. "But anytime you want to make an offer—great."

"Might as well," shrugs Sam after Betsy leaves. "We need to live somewhere."

"Even if this isn't our dream house," I say. "We can always move."

Eight days past my due date, we hire an inspector to come around and examine the pipes, the wires, the dirt cellar, and the crawl-through attic. He taps walls, lifts carpet corners, cranes his neck to peer at the roof and the gutters. He reaches the same conclusion about our dwelling as the sonogram technician reaches about my womb: "Looks good. No major problems."

Nine days past my due date, Betsy comes over and we draft an agreement on the back of an envelope. We drink more ice water. We shake hands. Sam puts his mouth to my belly, rests it on my floral-print blouse. "You can come out now," he laughs. "We've bought you a house."

Sam and I go out for Chinese food, the new-wives tale for bringing on labor that is really an excuse to have one more dinner out before the baby arrives. We sit in a red vinyl booth at Mary Chung. "Spicy food," I say. "Isn't that supposed to do the trick?" We order cold noodles in pungent sesame sauce and an extra serving of hot mustard.

"To the new house," Sam raises his beer glass.

"To the new baby," I toast.

We are celebrating homeownership: the end of throwing away rent money, the beginning of fixing things up as we please, a stake in the future, a nest, the fact that our life together has added up to something.

"I found it!" Sam exclaims. "Four years ago it was *me* who found our house. That was one thing I did right, wasn't it?"

"It was a great thing," I say. "I was ready to move into that dismal apartment on Pearl Street!"

"When I was a kid," he says, "my parents never once praised me. Never in their eyes did I do anything praiseworthy."

I cringe, as I always do when Sam offers these cruel bulletins from his childhood. A maternal sympathetic flash darts from my breast. I want to make it up to him. I want to soothe and praise the child he was, the child he never was.

"What about this?" I say, and touch my belly. "Isn't this something right?"

"Except I didn't have much to do with it beside signing a piece of paper to release my sperm," he muses.

It's true. After Sam banked his sperm prior to radiation treatment, impregnating me was a rather bodiless act. His legal signature was required to release the frozen vials from the bank to my clinic, where a technician inserted a single sperm into my egg.

"It's a good signature," I say. "Besides, think of all the women who wanted it."

Sam laughs. Between the time of his radiation and the time he and I moved in together, several single women expressed interest in his genetic material. He couldn't quite hand it over, he's told me, to that acquaintance in San Francisco. Hearing the woman's proposal over the phone—no strings attached, whatever paternal arrangement he wanted—made him realize that he'd rather keep his genetic material close. He'd rather have a relationship with the mother. He'd father his own child.

And now I slurp sesame noodles with the great gusto of my pregnancy. I look at my husband across the Formica table, head bent to his plate. His face never changes; always that handsome, bearded Semitic look. But in his voice tonight I sense reluctance and fear. He wants this baby, no doubt about that, but all through my pregnancy he's voiced his ambivalence. He'll write fewer books; he'll have less peace and quiet; we'll have less time, no freedom, more bills. And, always, the unspoken one: How long will he be around to be a father? Will he get sick?

With every pound I gained, with every inch the fetus grew, I was aware that Sam's body, too, was changing, except that his cells were dividing as they should not. My baby's cells are multiplying into life while my husband's cells are multiplying toward death. And now the show's almost up. Since we've returned from Paris, the last two months—the baby dropping, his head pressed against my cervix a continual reminder of his impending arrival— I've felt insulated from the fear of Sam's possible death. People die every day. Women die in childbirth. This other event, birth, blots out everything.

Ten days past my due date, a Friday, my OB calls me in. I lie down on the brown leather bed reserved for monitoring the fetal heartbeat. She straps a metal disc around my belly. I'm to lie on my side, hooked up to a machine that will record the baby's heartbeat. She whisks out of the room, skirt flouncing, promising to return in five minutes.

I'm anxious now, about the big event that has not yet happened. Besides, as a first-time pregnant lady, I am scared. Terrified, actually. I know that the mother's cartilage softens in late pregnancy, to allow the hip and pelvic bones to spread and give way, and that the cervix opens to ten times its usual size to let the baby out, but I cannot get over the fear that birth will split me open, like a peach pitted and halved. In a sense, my fears are correct. Not about childbirth, but about the months and years to come, when my marriage is split open, its center removed.

Dr. Noble returns. She lifts the ticker tape from the monitor and I see her chest heave, hear her stifle a gasp. Too quickly, she hastens to my side, shows me the black line that traces my baby's heart, beat by beat. I'm having tiny contractions, which is good, she assures, but there, where the line darts back instead of forward, is when the heartbeat slows. Decelerates. "Nothing alarming enough to warrant an emergency," she says, her voice wavering. Too quickly, she looks at her watch. Friday afternoon. "Let's check you in to the hospital right away," she says. "I'm making the call. Let's get this baby out."

I use Dr. Noble's phone to call Sam at his office. My legs are trembling as I repeat the OB's words. "Nothing alarming enough to warrant an emergency," I say to Sam. The line sounds dead. Silence on his end. "Sam? Are you there? Did you hear what I said?"

"I'll meet you at home in twenty minutes," he replies, his voice low and measured. "I don't like the sound of this."

At home, I grab the overnight bag I packed weeks ago. Nervous with energy, I sweep the kitchen floor, pace the front hall. Isn't walking supposed to bring on labor? I have held on too long, I see now, wanting to possess this infant only for myself when I have to let him out into the world. A slowed heartbeat. A slowed. A slow. I am worried, waiting for Sam.

I call my friend Lauren. She is supposed to be at the birth. At least that's the plan we concocted months ago. I was afraid then that Sam would not be present for the birth. Nothing tangible, really. He'd get sick prematurely. Or he'd bellow at the nursing staff, thinking me slighted, the care insufficient. Or his own anxiety about upcoming fatherhood would get the better of him. In any case, back in the fifth month of my pregnancy, when I voiced these fears to Lauren, she offered to be my birth advocate. Not a midwife or a birth *doula*, per se, but a friend on the scene.

"Hi," I tell Lauren now over the phone. "I just came back from being fetal monitored. The baby's got a decelerating heartbeat."

"I've heard of that," she says. "It's pretty common, I think."

"We're not taking any chances," I say, a little heatedly. "We're leaving for the hospital. They're going to induce."

"Right now? I have one more client to see today."

"Want to meet us when you're done?" I'm half-hoping she'll say yes and half-hoping she'll say no. Yes, because I know how much Lauren wants to be present at a birth and because, theoretically, the more friends a laboring woman has, the more support. No, because I'm beginning to sense just how very intimate is this journey that Sam and I are taking together, the journey of becoming parents.

"Of course I'll be there!" Lauren exclaims. "You know I don't want to miss this."

It's six in the evening when Sam and I check in at the triage desk at the birth center. Before I can be admitted to the medical area, I am taken aside by a social worker. Quietly, she fires a list of questions: "Do you have any reason to believe you are HIV positive?" No. "Do you need information about food stamps, Women and Infants Center?" No. "Do you have any reason to fear going home with the man who brought you here?"

Of course I say no to this last question, but as I do so I feel the slightest quiver of my lower lip. Although I do not fear going home with the man who brought me, I do fear what we will have to face soon after we go home. I want to ask if there is a box on her chart for Sudden Husband Death. I want to ask this careworn social worker, a woman with deep creases under her eyes, if there are statistics to support the poet Rilke's line that death and life are one at the core. Isn't that what happens every day at a large hospital? Death and life, life and death. How many are coming into the world and how many are leaving? There must be someone tallying the score. Here, six floors up, I can feel the building faintly throb with the arrival and departure of human souls.

Not Dr. Noble but another doctor from her practice is here to check my vital signs. I lie back on the chilly exam bed. On goes the gooey plastic of the fetal monitor. Dr. Lin takes my pulse, looks at her watch and then at the baby's heart measurements. "Mmnnn," she says. She is freckled and brown, relaxed in a loose-fitting smock, not at all like the crisp, belted skirts that the efficient Dr. Noble usually wears. "Looks pretty good right now," smiles Dr. Lin. "I'm not sure I would induce."

"This afternoon the heartbeat was decelerating," says Sam. He sounds harsh, challenging the doctor's judgment.

"These things change from hour to hour," replies Dr. Lin. "It's hard to say."

"Well, we're here," I say. "We'd rather not go home right now." All of a sudden I am tired of waiting for this baby to be born. The suspense is too heavy. Despite my intoxication with my pregnant state, I can no longer bear to have the thing not happen that is supposed to happen. And Dr. Noble has me worried, too.

"All right," says Dr. Lin. "I'll put you on prostaglandin gel. That's our first step induction. Thins the cervix. Sometimes it's enough to get things going." She looks at her watch. "Dr. Noble is coming on call in another hour. You'll be in her care."

Dr. Lin makes a notation on my chart, then leaves, trailing a gardenia scent.

Lauren arrives. She is beaming, excited. She perches on the doctor's round stool. She looks from Sam's downcast face to my languid body on the bed. "What's going on?"

I explain about the heartbeat. First, it was decelerating. Now, it is normal. We don't know.

"I want this watched," says Sam. "I don't like this."

"Decelerating heartbeat," says Lauren. "Happens all the time. Didn't you tell me the placenta deteriorates when the baby's overdue?" she says to me.

I shake my head. I don't remember saying that.

"But you did!" she insists. "No one's talking distressed fetus, right? How bad can it be?"

Lauren talks as if she knows, but she is not yet a mother, nor is she an obstetrician. Sam, who expects the worst in medical matters, perturbs me, but I'm also bothered by Lauren's breezy dismissal of our concerns. This is my real live baby we are discussing, not some abstract obstetrical case.

Dr. Noble parts the curtain. Thank goodness. She reads Dr. Lin's notes, shakes her head, looks at me, smiles, and says, "I'm on call all weekend. Maybe this baby was waiting for me!"

I scoot down the bed until my feet fit into the potholder-covered stirrups. Dr. Noble examines me. "Still only a centimeter dilated," she says. "Stay right there a minute. I'm going to get the gel."

My room is ready now, and we all three—me, Sam, Lauren—file down the hall from triage. From my overnight bag I unpack my favorite nightshirt, a golden-colored long T-shirt. During the fertility treatments I grew to hate the thin cotton hospital johnnies. I was always shivering. The little ties were always unraveling. My skin took on a pasty, institutional pallor. As a result, the main item on my birth plan is to Wear My Own Clothing. I slip my nightshirt on over my head now, delighting in the soft cotton and the scoop neck.

Lauren and Sam bounce around on the furniture in the room, turning on and off the light switches, like two toddlers, but I am here for the serious work of labor. I walk the halls. Around and around I go, on a long march. I pass the Chinese couple from our birthing class, she leaning into his side, her face pale as the walls. He looks up when I say hello. She tries to smile but grimaces instead. Clearly, they are unreachable, already in another zone, and soon to deliver. Not me. I am on a hike. For over an hour I walk, but still I feel nothing. No contractions, no cramping, no pain, no progress.

Dr. Noble gives the orders to "pit" me. Pitocin. It's nine-thirty.

A nurse with straggly dirt-blond hair and smeared orange lipstick hooks me up to an IV. In the back of the room, she adjusts dials, checks tubing. She straps the fetal monitor back on me. I'm to wear this contraption all through labor, call her to unhook it should I need to go to the bathroom.

"So much for the labor exercises," I say. In birth class we learned about walking, crouching, stretching, breathing, massaging. All of which require one to move about freely. Now I am attached to an electrical cord, my movements curtailed.

"At least we'll know how the baby's doing," says Sam. He walks over to the machines, pokes around looking for the one that shows the heartbeat.

"Prints out in the nurses' station," says the nurse, perfunctorily, snapping the chewing gum in her mouth. "We'll keep an eye out."

"Keep an eye out!" screams Sam.

I look at Lauren, her eyes growing wide. This is it. Sam's about to lose it. Watch.

"Excuse me," says Sam, his voice turned nasty. "Could you get a doctor back in here? I want a straight story about what kind of danger my child is in. What are the risks? What precautions are being taken? We've been given the runaround since we got here! Get Dr. Noble!"

The nurse sighs, snaps her gum louder. "All right," she says. "I'll page Dr. Noble."

Lauren runs out of the room, following the nurse. I am half-lying, half-sitting on the bed. Sam is pacing the floor, his voice rising to near-hysteria. "This is terrible! This could be tragic! Maybe we should go straight for a C-section. Are the drugs harming the baby? I thought we were going for natural childbirth!"

For once, I let him do his dance. I feel too heavy to respond. Also, a part of me is relieved he is making such a fuss. I see how important and dear this baby already is to him. I see how Sam and I share what no one else can—the unshakeable belief that nothing in all the world is more urgent than our baby's safety.

And there's another reason I am not bothered by his histrionics. Clearly, he fears his own heart slowing in the not too distant future. We both do.

It takes a long time for Dr. Noble to arrive. She's been helping the Chinese couple deliver. "They wanted you to know they had a girl," she tells us. Sam and I are resting, me on the bed, him on a chair. Lauren has returned from dinner at the cafeteria. "Give them our congratulations," Sam says. For a moment we all bow our heads in wonder at the new baby girl.

Dr. Noble tells us she's checked the heart monitor records and the baby is still safe. No fetal distress. Let's wait and see if I respond to the pitocin. "Get some rest now," she orders. "While you still can."

"Nothing's going to happen for awhile," I say to Lauren. "It's late. Why you don't you go home. We'll call you when the baby's coming."

"Really?" she says, sounding disappointed at losing a front row seat. "You want me to go?"

"There's nothing to do here. It must be boring for you."

"I wouldn't mind getting some sleep," she says.

"We'll call you," Sam says firmly. He's calmed now, by Dr. Noble's visit. "We'll call when we need you."

I lie on the bed, on my left side, and doze. I am thankful to be blanketed in such calm, such quiet. Sam folds out the chair for dads, takes off his shoes, and he too dozes. Dimly, I am aware of the straggly-haired nurse coming and going, ratcheting up the dials, adjusting the beep-beep-beep of the machines. I float in my own rich darkness. For the last time, the baby and I sleep as one.

I awaken with a jolt. I have been punched in the gut. How dare anyone inflict this band of pain across my belly? I am out of bed, my bare feet on the cold floor, undulating with a contraction. "Sam!" I yell. Moments later, the pain wave begins again. I grip the bed rail, try to sway into the band of pain. Sam is up, at my side, rubbing my back, commanding me to breathe, breathe, breathe.

"Can't you see how what we learned doesn't help?" I snap at him. "It's the pitocin. No buildup. Just these . . ."—I twist as I feel the next one coming—"megacontractions."

He keeps rubbing my back. "A hot washcloth," I tell him. "I need one."

When Sam returns from the sink in the corner, I order him to place the hot white towel on the small of my back. He lifts my shirt and complies. "Like this? Like this?"

"Yes," I say. "That helps." And, for a moment, I feel the pain dissolving, dulling to an oozing ache.

Again and again for what seems like ages, Sam shuttles back and forth from sink to bed, bringing me hot washcloths that are wrung and steaming and offer me, each time, momentary relief. "Again!" I snap. "More." We are like a relay team: he at the sink, me riding out the contractions, the baby dropping and dropping, nearly ready.

And then even the hot cloth will not help. I am bursting. All I can think about is how much I need to walk to the bathroom, but I cannot move with the monitor strapped on and hooked up. "Get the nurse!" I scream to Sam. "Right now!"

While he is gone, a tidal wave contraction hits hard. I am gagging, spitting up, juices spurting from my throat. I am frozen to this spot on the floor. The band of pain constricts tighter and tighter.

The nurse hands me a plastic bowl for my spit. She unhooks me from the machines, and slowly, on Sam's arm, I make my way to the bathroom. I close the door. The mother beast wants to be alone.

And then everything is coming out of me: spit, urine, shit, tears, sweat. I am not splitting open, as I feared, but there is so much I must release. Just when I think it's over, and I lean my hot cheek against the cool tile wall, I feel another surge. I never knew so much could pass through me. I am letting go, and go, and go. Letting go of my pregnancy, letting go of my childlessness, letting go of whoever I was until this hour. Letting go of Sam and I as a twosome. Letting go of things I cannot name. Air. Matter. Spirit.

When I have nothing left to release, I bend to wash my face in the sink. The cool water is so sweet. I dab my wrists and neck as if with a rare perfume. I step back into the birthing room.

The nurse wants to hook me up again to the machine, but I buck like an angry mare. I pull my wrists away. "No!" I snort. "I can't do that again. I have to walk freely."

I see Sam flattened against the wall, his expression one of complete horror.

I remain rooted to the floor in the middle of the room, the pain band contracting me again, my eyes closed so that I see tiny bright stars against my lids, and the word "mother" comes to mind. *Mother.* Hundreds of thousands of times I have said the word "mother," but always as a daughter, the image of my own mother attached. *My* mother. *My* mother says. *My* mother wants. *My* mother loves. Now the word "mother" vibrates with new meaning. *Mother.* That's me. Such an obvious thought, but at this moment it startles my whole body as a revelation.

"All right," says the nurse. "I'll call the doctor to check you."

Dr. Noble sails in, and for her I lie nicely on the bed. She pulls out her gloved hand. "Good work," she says. "Six centimeters. You can have the epidural now."

The epidural physician speaks with a singsong Indian accent. He wheels in his cart and right away, from the cajoling, comforting way he speaks to me, I see he is the drug dealer of this place. He promises to put an end to my searing pain. He will save me from beastliness. He will usher in a sweet birth.

I feel Sam's two strong hands on either side of my back, holding me steady. I feel myself leaning into his grip with the feeling that he is all I have just now. He is watching the doctor, I know, and making sure the needle goes correctly into my spine.

One jab, two jabs—"There," says Sam in his most soothing voice. "It's all over."

I lie back on the bed, and then the room slowly clears. Gone are the dancing stars and the bucking horse. Gone are my existential discoveries. Gone is the consuming pain. I am back. I am a woman having a baby, my husband at my side.

Dr. Noble returns. I look at the clock on the wall. It's six in the morning. Time to start pushing, she says brightly. Almost time.

My new, day nurse is jovial, patting me on the knee, smiling, encouraging. She wears cat's-eye glasses, their frames splattered with the colors of the sunrise.

Sam is hovering by me. Something in him has lifted and shifted, too; I feel him warm me like sunlight. Gently, he touches my neck, my flushed face, as if transferring his current.

All of a sudden I remember: "Lauren," I tell Sam. "We were supposed to call her."

Dr. Noble takes a deep breath. Sam and I hesitate. "Do you want . . ." he says.

"Do you?"

He thinks for a moment. Dr. Noble is waiting. "Not really," he says. "This feels like just us."

It's what I'm feeling, too. Between Sam and me this night, things have passed—hot washcloths, worries for the baby, pain and spit—that bind. He has witnessed me in such an extreme state! He has proven, in a new way, his devotion. Besides, the baby is pressing upon us. There is really no time.

"Okay," I say, "don't call her." As I say this, I feel bad that I am disappointing my friend, but my choice is clear. Right now it's Sam and the baby and me.

Dr. Noble steps in to take one of my bent legs, Sam and the nurse take the other leg. Together, they pace me. Push, says Sam.

Push, says Dr. Noble. I push, but rather ineffectively. I can't feel anything, and this, I guess, is what people mean when they talk about an epidural not allowing one to experience birth.

I push, or try to push, and Sam stands vigil, waiting for his first glimpse of the baby's head. His eyes open wide. I can see he is impressed by how large I've dilated. Dr. Noble asks if I want a hand mirror. "Do you want to see the baby's head emerge?"

"No thanks," I say. It's enough that Sam will witness this gloriously gory sight. There are some things about my body I do not need to know. Sam will.

Dr. Noble is patient. She tells me to push harder. She glances at the clock: seven-thirty in the morning. She'll let me go a little longer.

"Do you think there's meconium?" I ask her, worried about the danger of the baby ingesting fetal poop.

"Probably," she says. "By now. That's what may have been causing the slowed heartbeat."

"Will the baby be all right?"

"Probably." Her lips tighten.

"You have girls?" I ask Dr. Noble, for some reason thinking of the photographs of two little girls with blond ponytails in her office.

"Two girls and a boy," she says.

"That's a lot of kids," I say.

She nods. In a flash, I see Dr. Noble the mother, there on the stool. She has been up all night. She looks too thin, too tired, wisps of hair coming undone from her clip. Head bent forward, arms hanging loose at her side, she says quietly: "The third one put me over the edge."

"My grandfather was a doctor," says Sam. "In Chicago. He was in the first graduating class of the University of Illinois Medical School."

"We have some of his old equipment," I add. I tell Dr. Noble about the heavy, rusty speculum that Sam and I found in the family storage unit his mother rented. It looked medieval. Torturous, like an instrument made for tearing down vinyl siding.

"He did everything," says Sam. "Babies, old people—never took money from people who couldn't pay."

Dr. Noble nods. Those were the old days of medicine. Generalists. Home visits. The good, saving doctor.

And then, it's strange, but I feel a new presence in the room, one that's wise and benevolent, Sam's beloved relative. And what's even stranger, I think, is my conviction that this talk is not merely to pass the time but somehow necessary to the birth.

Dr. Noble glances at the clock. Let's push a little more. She and Sam take my legs again. "Oh!" says Sam.

"No," says Dr. Noble. The baby's head is appearing, only to disappear. He's coming out and then thinking better of it. Time for forceps, Dr. Noble declares.

And then, and then—I feel a tremendous whoosh and hear a snapping suck. People in white coats rush into the room. One of them carries my baby across the room. All I can see are my baby's flapping arms, like a prehistoric creature taking flight.

The baby is being cleaned, I know, cleared of meconium before he takes his first breath. Sam is across the room, and I am so relieved that he will watch over our baby these first few seconds in the world when I cannot.

The cat's-eye nurse sees me straining, worrying. "Those waving arms are a good sign," she says. "Sick newborns don't wave their arms."

Dr. Noble is stitching me up. She is watching me watch for my baby. She is so calm, pulling her thread, attending, that I too feel at peace. And then Sam comes over to me and I can tell from his half-smile and his buoyant step that the baby is fine.

The cat's-eye nurse hands me a tiny bundle wrapped in white cloth. He is so warm! How perfectly he fits in the crook of my arm! His eyes are so alert, and they are, I notice with awe and delight, an amazing purplish blue. We look and look at each other with such recognition. *Oh. It's you.* Does the newborn see his whole life stretching before him—the splendor and the grief, the tedium and joy, good fortune and bad, and most of all, the love? For I see, as I hand our bundle over to his eager new dad, how my whole life and Sam's whole life, and the union of our two lives, have led us all to this rare moment.

At least Sam gets to be here for this, is what flashes through my muddled mind. At least Sam is here with me today, to hold his two-minute-old son. At least Sam gets to push the telephone buttons in wild euphoria and proclaim our news to everyone we know. At least Sam gets to count Isaac's ten tiny toes and fingers.

"Let's talk numbers," he says on Isaac's first day in the world. He is standing by the window in the hospital room, cradling the baby close to his chest. "You are one. Your mom and I are two. Together, we are three."

In the afternoon, my parents arrive. They bring flowers. Speechless and beaming, they hold the sleeping baby. My brother and his wife arrive and my brother brings in extra chairs from the hallway and they all four sit in a semicircle around my bed, passing around the baby, exclaiming how cute he is and does he have my father's nose?

I feel so gratified to bring my son into this family, where I know he will be loved and treasured. "He already knows how to nurse," I boast. "Took right to it. See his mouth opening?" Isaac is six hours old and already I know his little ways better than anyone else does.

"He's a smart one," says my sister-in-law. "I can tell." She cradles him in the crook of her arm, gently rocking.

"And adorable," says my mother.

"And sweet," I say. "Give him back. I think he's hungry."

Sam is sweet too, this first day, practicing with the nurses how to swaddle an infant, tucking in the arms just so. I lean on him when I take my first, unsteady steps to the bathroom, the drugs not yet worn off, and he hands me my toothbrush and shampoo, fussing over me, making sure I have enough towels, assuring me that while I'm in the shower he'll watch over the baby, asleep again in his plastic bassinet. "I think Isaac's going to like numbers," he tells me, straight-faced.

I roll my eyes. "How can you tell?"

"I just can."

After I shower, I am ravenous. Sam talks to someone in the kitchen and a plate piled high with eggs and waffles and toast and fruit arrives. I devour everything.

"Better get some rest while you can," says Sam. Yes, I nod, obedient to this husband now who seems to have such a sense of what I need. He wheels Isaac in his bassinet down the hall to the nursery.

When I wake, I see a card propped on my bedside table: "Congratulations! He's perfect! I wore my pink shirt today because pink is the color of love. Aunt Gerdy."

Forty-eight hours later, Sam and I are struggling to figure out how to put the car seat into the car. I'm holding Isaac. Sam is leaning into the backseat, threading the seatbelt through various plastic openings. "Two Ph.D.'s," he groans, "and we can't even figure out the damn car seat."

I've dressed the baby in a cotton sleeper printed with ducks. He's sucking on a pacifier and is as calm as a Buddha, as if prepared for whatever comes next. I look straight into his blue eyes. "We're taking you home, little guy," I whisper. "You'll see. You'll like it."

"Got it," pronounces Sam, emerging from the car. "At least I think so."

He places his hand beside mine beneath Isaac's soft wobbly head, and together we buckle the baby into the car seat. I sit in the backseat too, wanting to keep a close watch.

There's a lot of traffic on Brookline Avenue to maneuver, and Sam glides skillfully, slowly, carefully. We have a baby on board. We are entrusted with this new being who is wholly dependent on us. I'm sitting on a pillow, but still I wince at every bump, feeling the burn of my episiotomy. We stop at a red light. I look out the window at the cars, everyone going somewhere. Beside us is a blue minivan, a woman with streaked and flyaway hair at the wheel. She is singing along with the radio, bouncing her head, but I can't make out the words. Up further I see a white Pontiac with two Hassidim in the front seat, the two men staring straight ahead, their jowls sweaty in the heat, their eyes burning with righteousness. And there's a man on a motorcycle, his helmet fluorescent. And over there's the old Peter Fuller Cadillac building, and Boston University spewing notebook-carrying students down Commonwealth Avenue, and the bridge over the river Charles, its green waters flowing to the Atlantic. The city is throbbing today in the summer heat. So many lives! So many roads! That a baby was just born to Sam and me feels so extraordinary. *I just had a baby! I had a baby!* I want to shout to the stalled shoppers in their Mercedes. Instead, my eyes fill with warm tears. ✦

PART 2

THE BARGAIN

"Being ill and dying is largely, to a great degree, a matter of style."

— *Anatole Broyard,* Intoxicated by My Illness

5

DELIRIOUS

The first day home with our new baby, Sam brings me a tall
green glass and a silver pitcher filled with cold, clear water.
All day and all night I drink away my voracious thirst, and when
the pitcher is empty, he fills it again. All day and all night the
baby nurses, and when he cries, I lift him again to my breast. I
have an inflatable plastic doughnut to ease the pain when I sit,
and ice packs and pads and a container of Tucks, and bottles of
iron pills and Tylenol, and a new baby who wants to be held and
fed. I am mother and recovering patient both.

Not that I mind the physical discomfort. Just now, the world
is like a gift. This healthy baby with a steady gaze and grip, warm
in my arms, who will heal my womb with his strong suck. The
UPS man rings our bell daily to deliver doll-size outfits decorated
with blue bunnies and bears, a silver rattle, *two* copies of *Good
Night Moon*, a tremendous blooming bouquet, a Pierre Cardin
fleece bunting, a soft doggy with raggedy legs. Besides these literal presents, I count as gifts: a glow emanating from the orange

mohair blanket, the cool touch of the silver pitcher, and the un-
mistakable sensation that wherever I am, I can hear majestic
chords playing—a postpartum music of the spheres.

Sam, my husband, the father of my child, is a gift. He makes
me grilled cheese sandwiches, for which I have a particular
craving, and takes the baby while I eat. He balances the baby
along his arm, and something about his sure hold along the baby's
head and the contrast between smooth, tiny, vulnerable baby and
rough, muscular, strong man makes my heart well up.

The morning of the bris, a Sunday in late September, is bright
and fair, one of the last warm days, the kind of weather that New
Englanders tell themselves to enjoy before the cold winter ahead.
My bedroom window is open, and the baby and I sit in a gentle
breeze listening to the clatter downstairs that is Sam and my
mother and Sam's brother Alan, who flew in from Israel, and
cousin Bonni, who flew in from L.A., fixing platters of bagels and
cream cheese and whitefish and lox. I can smell my mother's
sugary plum cake cooking in the oven. The sharp aroma of fresh
coffee. Freshly mown grass.

I kiss the baby's warm crown. "It's your big day," I whisper.
"This is all for you."

I am what people call a calm and confident new mother. True,
this first week home with a newborn has introduced me to sleep
deprivation, engorged breasts. . . . Yet I am lucky in that Sam
made sure I have plenty of support right from the beginning, and
this has made new motherhood that much easier. Together, he

and I fumble through our first diaper changes: new dad holding Isaac on the table, new mom turning the diaper around and around until she figures out where the paper tabs go. Sam orders tortellini and salad from our favorite neighborhood trattoria, then sets the table with candles and wine. We've arranged for a post-partum *doula* to come in three mornings. This fairy godmother fills the house with the aromas of roast chicken and lentil soup. She arranges fresh-cut flowers in a vase. She shows me how to hold Isaac across my palm so he doesn't slip when I give him a bath, how to place his bassinet near sunlight so he doesn't jaun-dice. She cares for the baby while I nap and shower. She sits by my side, coaching, while I learn how to nurse.

As if into a feather quilt, I am falling—gently, blissfully—into the idea of an uncomplicated future. A future, that is, where Sam will not fall ill. I allow myself to forget about the sword dangling so very close to my husband's head.

The doorbell rings. I hear Sam's hearty greeting and then footsteps on the stairs, and then a slight man wearing a blue button-down shirt bounces into our bedroom. Andrew, the pedi-atrician *mohel*, has arrived. I unlatch the sleeping baby from my breast and hold out his perfect length.

"Congratulations," says Andrew. I close my blouse, suddenly self-conscious with a man I do not know in my bedroom. I see him take in the pink bloom on my cheek, the milky pallor of my skin.

Carefully, Andrew peels back my son's diaper. "A good one," he says, making light of the moment. "Straight up and down."

He sits on the edge of the bed to administer Tylenol drops into Isaac's mouth. "I have two," he tells me. "A nine-year-old girl and a six-year-old boy."

"Oh," I say, interested, listening. This is new for me, a parent-to-parent chat. I am being taken into the fold. "I have just one piece of advice for new parents," Andrew says. "Make time for each other. My wife and I have a standing dinner date every Saturday night. Keeps us connected."

I feel my stomach tighten. If only it were that easy! If only Sam's and my problems could be smoothed over by regular dinner dates! But for this moment at least, I too relish the illusion that Sam and I will adjust easily to our changed status. I nod in agreement. What good advice. We'll keep it in mind.

The doorbell rings again and again and I hear the house fill with the merry greetings of our guests. Sam has promised to do everything today. I am to rest upstairs with the baby until the ceremony begins. My door open, I recognize cousin Arleen, flown in from Wilmette. I hear Sam's old gang—Miranda, Willy, Mitchell, Naomi—whom we haven't seen for months and months but who have come out full force for this celebration. I had no idea so many would come—I am touched. I am touched, too, that Sam organized this event. Sam, whom I heard talking and talking on the phone this past week, his voice musical with pride, while I lay in bed, my gaze locked into Isaac's.

The time comes for me to descend our spiral staircase, babe in arms. I'm fully dressed for the first time in eight days—jeans and my favorite print maternity blouse. Dangly silver earrings. Sandals. Standing at the top of the stairs, unsteady, dizzy, I am struck, as if by an ocean gale, by the crowd looking up. My brother Ken, Pagan, Harvey, Patricia, Julie and Jeff, Lenny and Shoshana, Ann, cousin Lena. Their faces are shining. Has Sam spiked the punch? How else to explain this love rushing up the stairs? Most of our friends know how hard we worked to have this baby, but few know that we fear Sam's illness returning. Once again, I fall into the feather comforter. Our child is a miracle. Our child is a celebration.

I walk into the crowded dining room and over to my dear husband. His eyes are glistening. He puts one arm around the baby and me and the other arm around his old friend Charlie, here from Highland Park. Charlie bends over Sam, kisses me on the cheek. "Mazal Tov," he says.

Cousin Arleen swoops down, coos, "Oooh, how beautiful!" and scoops up the baby. "Thanks for coming," I say, and laugh. "You look great!" Which she does: every hair in place, large gold hoops, pressed blue suit. "I had to be here," she says, looking adoringly at the baby. "For Mildred." I think of Sam's mother and how proud she would be on this day. *Arleen will tell her all about it* is what flashes through my sleep-deprived mind, as if Arleen and Mildred, who spoke on the phone nearly every day of their adult lives, still have a special line.

Mildred died on Thanksgiving Day, ten days after Sam and I were married in City Hall and three weeks after her friend Rabin's assassination. A Palm Springs police officer found her fallen on the bathroom floor, beside her vanity table. She was fully dressed and made up, ready to go out. A cardiac arrest.

Sam and I flew out to Palm Springs and then flew with the body back to Chicago, where Mildred lived the majority of her life and where she was to be buried. About five hundred people came to her funeral. As he had done at his father's funeral ten years before, Sam spoke of his parents' achievements. Mildred was the only woman besides Golda Meir to be recognized as Man of the Year by the Israel Bond Organization; she was the literary editor of a Chicago daily and a well-known book reviewer in her youth; she was the youngest president of any Hadassah organization in the country. . . . He did not talk about any devotion to her children because there was little to say. Later, he told me that his parents' act was a tough one to follow and that he had chosen not to do so.

At the funeral I was in the odd position of meeting Sam's extended family. "Congratulations on your marriage," said his aunts and cousins. And then, in the next breath: "We're so sorry."

We did not have a wedding party in May, as planned. As newlyweds, by Sam's request, we went into a year of mourning, as prescribed by Jewish tradition. This was a somber, inward time, one where we shunned celebration. Now, with the birth of our son, it is time to celebrate. Alan's tall form hovers close, the click-click-flash of his camera going off.

The room is so packed with people that it's almost impossible to turn without bumping into someone. Here is my mother pressing me close with a hug, her body warm and welcoming, and my Aunt Gerdy besides, also hugging me, so that I must squirm into a standing position between them, one arm around each sister, holding on to them and holding them up with equal pressure.

Sam, Alan, and my father, their arms taut and stretched tall, pass Isaac above the crowd and across the room. I feel safe about my son, seeing him literally supported by the men. Are not his father, uncle, and grandfather showing him the beauty of motion and the ease of great heights? They carry him, wide-eyed, in an arc, as our guests raise their heads to see the child that has been born; and then, as if at the end of a long-held-in breath, the men deposit Isaac into his car seat, which rests on the dining room table.

Sam steps forward to give his speech. "Isaac means," he begins, "'one who laughs.' And so, with this name, dear son, we tell you that life is absurd and precarious, and fate is often dark, but we can always laugh—at all of it."

May our fate not be too dark, is what I silently pray.

Next the *mohel* and Charlie and Sam and Alan and my dad chant the traditional Hebrew prayers over Isaac. May he stay true to Torah, Mitzvah, and Chuppah—which Sam roughly translates as education, a life that helps to make the world a better place, and a good marriage.

And then Sam is beside me at the head of the table. He squeezes my shoulder; I lean into his side. It feels good and right to be standing together like this before a community of relatives and friends, as if in becoming parents at the bris of our eight-day-old son we are also wedding each other again, this time in public. A hush has fallen over the room. The room is so hot and so still. It is my turn to speak.

"I haven't prepared a speech," I begin, my voice a quavering whisper, "and really, this feels like too large a moment to contain." I look down at the floor, then back up at all these good people. "I wish for happiness and long life for my child," I say. "Health and safety and splendor and strength." And then, be it postpartum hormones or sleep deprivation or overwhelming joy, I just stand there with tears streaming down my face. "Thank you all for coming," I stammer. "Thank you for sharing this day with us."

And then it is time for the *mohel* to do what he came here to do. Alan guides my father up to the table, and I see that my father's face is white with fear. I leave the dining room and stand in the kitchen, my hands ready to cover my ears should the baby's screams tear too much at me. My mother joins me there in the kitchen. We have not had a bris in my family in two generations, and now my mother gives me a look that says: *How could you enter into this barbaric custom?*

"If you're going to circumcise," I say to my mother, trying not to sound didactic, "I'd rather do it with a party of love. Besides, the baby's older than he'd be in the hospital, where they strap him down."

By the silent way she straightens the food platters on the kitchen table, I can see that my mother is not convinced.

I believe what I say. I want my Isaac to be part of tradition that extends back to Biblical times, to have the strength of that tradition. The cutting of the foreskin is a sign of faith. Faith in the future, faith in life, faith in holding on and going forward. And I need that faith now, for even in celebration I cannot entirely forget the precariousness of Sam's condition.

From the dining room—sharp infant cries. I rush in.

"Mazal Tov," cry Sam and Alan and Charlie, their shouts nearly drowning out the baby's distress.

Andrew rests Isaac across his forearms and turns away with him for a private conversation. "I apologize for causing you pain," he says very seriously, looking down at the red-faced infant. "I'm truly sorry."

Then he hands my baby to me. "Mom," he says, "take him upstairs and feed him."

Our guests return to their homes, their lives. The UPS truck no longer screeches to a halt in front of our house. The *doula* helps out three more mornings and then she, too, is no longer necessary. We can feed and bathe and burp and change our baby. The temperature drops; frost falls at night; I unpack sweaters and coats. Change is in the air.

Change comes for us in the form of a thin white envelope slipping through the mail slot. I bend to pick it up, and even before I finish reading the return address—Massachusetts General Hospital—I know what it is. I bring the news to Sam. "Open it," I say.

Just a form letter. *Please schedule your annual appointment with me.* Below, in blue ink, Dr. Shipley has written: "Your PSA needs to be checked."

In the last two-and-a-half years, Sam's PSA had nearly doubled, alarming to me. This change made Sam refocus on his own mortality. He was alternately anxious and dismissive. But now, with the arrival of this note, which brings back the fears and suspicions we've managed to put aside, we are truly worried again. I swear I see an aura around Sam's body, and it is gloomy gray in color. "My life is over," he groans.

Some warble in his throat, some teetering in his balance, cues me that his is no simple melodrama of new fatherhood. Sam is not like a friend's husband who complained about the birth of their first child: *Life as we know it is over.* This other, entirely healthy, new father meant: *No more late nights out and Sunday mornings sleeping in.* Nor can Sam's woe be helped by the soothing advice of parenting books: *Give yourselves time to adjust.*

Sam's groan becomes a wail that echoes against the bedroom window. Head against the pillow, babe at my breast, I feel my breath shorten, because in this instant I know as clearly as I know the acrid scent of autumn that when Sam says "My life is over," he means it literally: *I have helped my son into the world and now I can leave it.*

And then begins a time when nothing I can do or say will comfort my husband. I have run out of words and gestures. Those first weeks home, Sam was alert to the baby's every change, but now half a day can pass and he will not be interested in whether the baby ate or peed or why he is crying. He no longer moves his finger to check if our son can track with his eyes. He is no longer selecting Mozart CDs to play while I nurse.

"Here," I say to Sam. I hold out Isaac. "Don't you want to hold him? Talk to him about numbers?"

"What's the point?" Sam mumbles. He turns away, sticks his hands in his pockets. "What's the use? I'm afraid to attach. I'm afraid to get close. It'll only make it more difficult if I have to check out. Too hard for me and for him."

Sam takes six weeks, to the end of the postpartum period. Then he gets his blood tested.

We wait.

We expect bad news.

We get good news: the baby's first, gummy smile.

We get bad news: The PSA has risen again, from 3.2 in May to 5.3 at the end of October. More than two points in five months. Dr. Shipley calls this "not quite satisfactory."

Sam is supposed to schedule a biopsy, presumably to confirm a cancer reoccurrence in the gland, but Dr. Shipley is vague about how soon this should occur. "What difference does it make?" Sam says, still gloomy. "If it's time to go, it's time to go."

"Goddamit, will you *do* something, before it's too late," I plead. "Schedule something. Talk to someone."

He shrugs, noncommittal. He opens the cupboard and removes a bag of Guiltless Gourmet corn chips.

"I hate your fatalism," I say. "I hate your passivity. I think you're in denial."

He puts a chip in his mouth. Nothing from him but a resounding crunch.

"If you get sick," I warn Sam, "I'll be taking care of everyone."

Suddenly, he swings toward me, alert, his pupils dilating.

"The baby comes first," he says. "If you have to make a choice about who to care for, Isaac is more important than me."

At night, in bed, Sam nudges me awake. He is drenched in sweat. "A nightmare," he stutters. "I dreamed I was holding a watch that was broken in two. Just smashed to pieces."

We do not analyze this dream, as is our habit. Its meaning is too obvious. He's running out of time, his life has been smashed in two. . . . Over the next several days, Sam stops wearing his watch altogether—a Swatch, with a plastic wristband that's decorated with scratch drawings of the planets.

I live in two distinct time zones. The first, baby time, is divided into short, intense, immediate intervals. Twenty-minute feedings on each breast, two hours between feedings, five-minute diaper changes, twelve-minute crying bouts, and three-hour naps. I sleep two hours, three hours, forty minutes, and convince myself that this is sufficient rest. Baby time is measurable. Isaac's arms grow fat, he learns to smile and then to laugh, his tummy jiggling. The onesie that swam on him upon coming home from the hospital is now stretched tight.

The other time zone in which I live is illness time. This time zone moves in long, slow, dreadful intervals. It's been six years since Sam was treated with radiation therapy, and now, in late December, two months have passed since the PSA came back "unsatisfactory." Another month passes before Sam musters up the courage to schedule a biopsy, only to be told that the urologist cannot see him for another ten days.

Always, we are waiting, expecting the worst. Sam balances our beautiful Isaac along the length of his arms. "I want to see you grow up," he whispers.

The first night that the baby sleeps not in his straw bassinet beside our bed but in his Winnie the Pooh–decorated crib, which is directly across the hall, a mere twenty feet away, I sit on the top stair and cry uncontrollably. I am surprised by my sorrow, for lately I have been such a stoic. I have become an Amazonian woman who can walk for miles through the city with a baby strapped to my gigantic breasts. I have an endless supply of milk. Every day I shield my child from countless dangers: sharp-toothed dogs, swerving buses, scalding water, cold floors, bright lights, rashes. And now I sit on the top step and cannot stop my hard, gushing sobs.

"Karen, Karen, it's okay," says Sam. He rests his hand on my shoulder. I can see he's surprised, too, even worried, by my outburst. "Isaac's fine. Didn't we agree . . . ?"

We'd agreed that since Isaac was now three months old and Sam, given the stress of likely illness, needed the calm of his bedroom back, sans diapers and blankies and binkies and rattles, and since people told us that the baby was a good age to move now—not so tiny to be in danger, not so old as to notice the change—we'd move him into his own room.

Except that now I am overcome by unexpected grief. It suddenly hits me, like a searing deep in my belly, that all life is some degree of postpartum, of separation after birth. Every event is a separation from this first union between mother and infant, when we shared nourishment, oxygen, and blood. How did my mother and I ever survive this tragedy? How will I survive it again with my son?

The distance between people just now feels unbearable. Tonight, Isaac sleeps in his own room. Now it is only a matter of time before he moves farther and farther away, first refusing to let me kiss him when I say good-bye at school, then not telling me things, then driving a car, and before long he'll sleep in his own dwelling, Sam, and me too, in the grave.

And then it is the grave I am crying about. Death, that final separation. I cannot bear death parting me from Sam.

"Karen, Karen, Karen," says Sam. He sits down beside me on the narrow step and I feel his solid warmth. He puts his arm around my shoulder. "It's going to be okay."

I strap Isaac into his car seat and we go out, to a group for new mothers.

I take a place on the floor, in the circle, and arrange Isaac so he is wedged between my leg and hip. Beside me is a woman dressed in baggy sweats with her scraggly hair pulled back in a scrunchy. She is gazing into the watery eyes of her moonfaced infant, but she turns her head to flash me a welcoming smile.

I give my attention to the circle of mothers. The woman speaking is wearing a long tie-dyed scarf slung across her front, a sling in which her baby lies. "First we tried the whole grain rice cereal. Gas. Then the regular brand oatmeal cereal mixed with water. She wouldn't let me get the spoon in her mouth. Brian tried; sometimes she does things for him she won't for me. Cried in her high chair. I called the pediatrician, who said, 'Let it go, wait a few more days and then try again.' And then, finally, this morning, I just turned on her favorite Raffi tape and I said to myself, this child is not going to starve. She knows what she needs. When she's ready to eat solids, she will. And she opened her mouth! Ate five spoonfuls!"

"Yeah!" says a woman across the circle. "See, she was ready."

"My doctor said to introduce solids one color at a time," says a woman wearing felt clogs. "First, orange and yellow, then green, and then fruits."

At first, I soak up every word. I love the indulgence of being nothing but a new mother. Certainly, I have agonized whether Isaac is eating enough. At home, where I often feel like a new mother married to a man with a death sentence, there are graver issues than the color of baby food. But soon I tire of listening to people talk so intensely about baby furniture, baby schedules, and baby poop. Please, I want to shout, isn't there anything else? My husband is dying!

Now we put the baby down at nine each evening. Then Sam and I spend our quality time together in our own room lying on top of our bed and watching TV—any show will do for our numb, sunken spirits. At eleven the baby wakes and I go into his room to feed, burp, change his diaper, and feed again until he drops back to sleep. Then I climb under the covers, beside Sam. I circle my arms around the smooth curve of his back.

"I'm just so fucking scared," Sam whispers into the dark. "I don't *want* to die. I don't *want* to leave you."

"Shhh," I say. "Don't worry. It's going to be okay, hon." With my fingers, I knead the knots from his back. I work the warmth back into his chilled body. Since my outbreak on the top of the stairs, I am once again a calm reservoir of strength. I am the nurturer, the giver—the mother. Back and forth my fingers poke, until we both breathe evenly into sleep.

At three in the morning I am startled from sleep by the baby's sharp cry. I bolt from bed, milk dampening the front of my nightshirt. Two steps, three steps, and I am across the hall, lifting Isaac from his crib, pulling him close to me, as together we fall onto the futon I keep made up on the floor. If I time it right, I can get Isaac's greedy mouth latched on, myself comfortable under the quilt, and keep both of us happy—him with suck, me with sleep.

Other nights, when I cannot fall back to sleep, I wander the house. I do not switch on a lamp. Tonight I need to be blanketed in darkness. I need to feel the wood banister's smooth curve beneath my palm, and the dining room door swing open to my gentle push. I am one with my house now. I open the refrigerator and by its light I pour milk and cereal into a bowl. I want nothing more now than to sit on the couch by the window and eat my seven-grain cereal, slowly.

Here, with no one else's demands to answer, I can think. For everything has changed in so short a time. Just three months ago I was still a mother-to-be. I did not doubt my ability to love and care for a child, but neither was I prepared for this wild emotion. No one told me how far I would fall in love, at age forty, when I'd resigned myself to being an old married woman, all that pulse-quickening excitement relegated to the past. No one told me about this soulful eye gazing, these hours-long deep embraces—this constant *flirtation* with my own son.

I must watch not to lose myself completely in the baby's sweetness. I can feel myself dissolving into dimpling baby flesh, baby love, baby care, until there is no Karen, no Sam, no cancer, no grief, only this myopic round of feedings and naps and diaper changes, only this tiny being whose fingers clench tight around mine, saying, Here, here, here. How blissfully he sleeps at my breast, his mouth puckered into an O, his breath so even. His body molds to mine. I tuck him under my arm and carry him around the house while I throw spaghetti into a pot, detergent into the washer. I am a monkey mother, carrying her young. I put him down on a blanket and he turns red-faced with cries. I pick him up and he is content. I am a powerful woman. I can make things right for this small person when I can make nothing right again for Sam.

I sleep with my husband only half the night now. In the morning, when he wakes, I must remember to return to him.

In the mother's group today, we are talking about husbands.

"Every night when he comes home from work, Peter gives Leora a bath," says Dina. That's *their* time. And my time to make dinner."

"I've been pumping, putting milk in the freezer. Then my husband can get up for the midnight feeding," says Alexandra.

What am I supposed to say? My husband won't take his turn with the baby because he has cancer? Toward him I feel I must be forgiving, understanding, accommodating. He's the one with the life-threatening disease. I only have sleep deprivation, aching breasts, and a dull gray sadness. "We just found out that my husband probably has cancer," I say. "I don't feel right demanding anything of him."

A hush falls over the group. Cancer. The word sounds harsh and unreal in this room full of thriving infants. Thank goodness the conversation shifts again, and now we are talking about sex. The husbands are clamoring for it, and the new mothers are not particularly interested.

"I worry," I say, "that I don't love my husband enough since the baby came. I feel guilty about it, divided in my loyalties. I'm afraid I'm leaving the marriage for my child. He is so beautiful and Sam, now, has become so difficult."

We hire a nanny: Rita Alexandrovich, formerly of Odessa, presently of Coolidge Corner. Four mornings a week Rita arrives by bus. She smells like clementines. She carries a large shoulder bag and from it pulls an endless stream of woolen caps, plastic rattles, windup toys that splutter and race across the floor. "Aaah," she says when I hand her Isaac. "How is our philosopher today? We will go to the park. Beneath the evergreen I will say for you a little Pushkin."

We fall under Rita's spell. For five hours I can do as I please. My first book has been accepted for publication, and I use the time to work on revisions. I take a shower, a nap. I meet a friend for lunch. I browse a bookstore. All this is heavenly.

What is not so heavenly is the amount of time I am spending with Sam in doctors' offices. For this is what we do together now. Consult with specialists. Worry and wait. Compose lists of medical questions. Schedule an MRI, a CAT scan, and a needle biopsy. Has the cancer spread to the pelvis, the bone, the spine? We are told this is entirely possible. We are mostly silent, each of us conserving our energy for what's absolutely necessary. We expect a long battle ahead with disease. We need each other to navigate the parking lots at the Dana Farber, the Mass General, the Beth Israel. Such powerful institutions are they! Walking the gleaming corridors, I feel how they pulse with knowledge and expertise. Yet we, who are parents now, responsible for another life that we have brought into the world, feel suddenly adrift, with no one to look after us. More specifically, no one to look after Sam. Dr. Shipley, the radiologist oncologist to whom Sam has looked for the past six years, can no longer help. Dr. Shipley has made referrals, suggested we seek several opinions. "A man with a cancer recurrence after radiation failure," he says, "is a difficult case, indeed."

I take the red line to Downtown Crossing. Winter's coming, and I'm shopping for a pair of boots. Outside of Filene's Basement, Santa is shaking his bell for the Salvation Army. When I was a child and shopped here with my mother, she always made a point to give coins for those she called "less fortunate than us." From this I understood that my life was fortunate. We were the givers, the grateful ones. Bad things happened to other people.

Now, out of habit and memory, I forage the bottom of my purse for change. I find two heavy quarters, a fluttering dollar bill. I make my drop in the bucket. Santa nods, and his cotton beard bobs up and down.

I walk in and out of stores, browsing and musing, looking for my boots. Everywhere I go I hear Santa's bell ringing, insistent, rhythmic, bored with salvation's job. Salvation will never end. He has stood on this same spot since I was a child, thirty years at least, and still there are countless souls to save.

Such a long time ago now since Sam came to dinner at my house in Jamaica Plain. That night I began the turn toward midlife when I took Sam's hand; every night since, dreaming beside him, I've continued that turn. Now, here I am, a forty-year-old woman seeking to reinvent myself. Here I am, absorbed in my son's birth and my husband's possible death. Here I am, in the middle of my life.

The boots I buy are rugged. They are lined with Thinsulate. Their soles have thick rubber traction. They will take me through snow, ice, water, and mud. I lace them up. I am ready to march.

The night before Sam's biopsy. Tomorrow morning, a sonogram-guided needle will be inserted up his rectum, and then ping, ping, ping, nine tissue samples will be taken from the four quadrants of his prostate gland. Sam tells me it doesn't much hurt.

"We've got to prepare ourselves," says Sam. "We've got to assume that the biopsy will be positive, cancer found. Why else would my PSA be so high?"

We are lying in bed. "How long before we hear about the results?" I ask.

"About a week."

"So we have ourselves another wait," I sigh.

"I've already booked an appointment with Scardino, in Houston."

Scardino is Dr. Peter Scardino of the Baylor Medical Clinic.

He is one of the few surgeons who will perform what's called a salvage radical prostectomy—removal of the prostate gland after radiation has already burned and scarred the tissues. Various doctors have told us that a salvage is too messy, too risky, and promises too low a success rate. But a salvage is our only hope for cure. Without it, the cancer will surely spread beyond the gland, metastasize into Sam's bones, and slowly, inevitably, destroy his body.

"And if he agrees to take you on?" I ask.

"His receptionist told me to expect at least a week's recovery in the hospital."

"I'll call," I say. "There must be a social worker who arranges places for out-of-town families to stay. At least it's warm in Houston this time of year. I'll speak to Rita. Maybe she'll come down too. To help with Isaac. I know it's expensive, but if this isn't the time to spend money, I don't know what—"

"Hon," says Sam. "It's too much trouble for you."

"What are you talking about? You can't do this alone. Someone has to be there."

"Well, let's not get ahead of ourselves. Let's see what Scardino says."

The biopsy is on a Monday. Tuesday, Wednesday, Thursday, Friday we wait to hear the results. On Saturday morning, the snow falls like latticework outside our living room windows. Isaac lies on a blanket on the floor. He coos with delight, and for the first time ever bats at the cloth toys that hang from the curved bars of his baby gym.

Sam and I sit on the floor, beaming at our progeny. He can reach! He can grasp! Surely, we tell each other, our boy is greatly gifted.

Yesterday, at the bakery, Isaac kicked with delight as he dangled from his carrier. He sang to the muffins and loaves. He fell in love with green frosted cupcakes and with the madeleines arranged on a plate. And the day before, he crooned to the square-patterned holes in the radiator grating. He was so fascinated with the floral print tablecloth in my mother's dining room that he stuffed it in his mouth. I am thinking of all this, thinking that my four-month-old child is teaching me just how many miraculous sights deserve song, when the phone rings.

"I'll get it," says Sam.

Isaac rolls over on his stomach, lifts his head like a seal.

I hear Sam say, "Good morning, Dr. Shipley."

He carries the phone into the living room. He lowers himself onto the couch. "Yes, yes, I understand," he says. "Yes, I certainly will take it as good news. Thank you."

He hangs up, stunned.

"What?" I say. "What did Shipley say?"

"The biopsy came back negative. No cancer present. Shipley says there is no reason to take action at this point. I'm going to cancel the Scardino consult."

My head feels light. I am giddy as I was as a girl when I heard that the snowstorm canceled school for the day and I was given a reprieve, a time of unexpected freedom. "No cancer?" I say, incredulous. "How is that? A rising PSA and a negative biopsy?"

Sam shakes his head. "Shipley doesn't understand it either. He just said there's no reason to do a salvage at this point. He wants me to schedule another biopsy in awhile."

"No trip to Houston? No operation? You mean you're okay?"

"For the time being, anyway."

I pick up Isaac and rock him on my shoulder. I feel the tension leaving my body. It is such a relief to be merely rocking a child and not rocking a child while worrying about my husband's health. "That's a miracle," I say.

"Or a medical quandary," says Sam. "Anyway, we're off the hook for now."

He reaches for the baby. He holds him close to his chest and glides across the carpet. Left, then right, he sashays. He and Isaac dip and turn. Around and around they go.

Lightly, easily, I step from the room. I work one woolen socked foot and then another into my all-weather boots, and tightly I lace them up. From the front hall closet I remove my coat, Sam's parka, and Isaac's snowsuit. I locate mittens and hats.

We take a walk up Sparks Street, where the two-hundred-year-old oaks grow tall and regal. The sidewalk is narrow; the snow is ankle deep. No one is out yet, not even the plow, and this white field is, for the moment, ours. Sam, walking with a new certainty, carries our singing son in the backpack. The flakes fall fast and powdery, sticking to eyelashes, cheeks, mittened hands, making us a snow family who will be glorious for a season, until spring comes and we melt.

Sam turns his head to tell me something. I skip to him, just a few steps, to catch his words before the cold does. ✦

6

THE BARGAIN

In the cab from LaGuardia, the wintry sun shining off the Hudson, Sam and I lace together our hands, holding on. His cancer has definitely returned.

The driver pulls up at a long building the color of bone. He parks behind a delivery truck. "Memorial Sloan-Kettering," he announces, as if we've arrived at a five-star hotel.

Inside, the lobby smells sour, as if the worn carpeting has soaked up the despair and grief of too many. A woman with a pink scarf tied around her head walks by, her eyes like two bullet holes. A wisp of a man shuffles by on crutches. A black man dressed in black leather boasts to a bald girl with a nose ring: "I went through a whole lot of hell to get to where I am today."

"Arlie?" says a forty-something woman into her cell phone. "Arlie! They got it all. There was nothing on the rims." And then she starts to weep.

"Oh God," I say to Sam. "We're really here. In the middle of this fucking disease."

We're really here, in December 1998, nearly a year since we received the unexpected news of Sam's negative biopsy. For months after Shipley's phone call, we understood this anomaly— a rising PSA with a negative biopsy—as either a medical mystery or a medical quandary. We felt blessed, and strangely spared. Curiously, no doctor challenged this belief. Dr. Shipley said only, "Get another biopsy in a couple of months." But his tone was casual, without urgency.

Sam postponed, put off, delayed. He was busy: being a new father, putting his mother's affairs in order, and writing a grant proposal. From time to time I prodded Sam to go get another PSA test, but truth be told, I wanted a respite between having a baby and having a husband in crisis. That first year of parenthood was so intense and absorbing and joyful that we couldn't quite bring ourselves to mar the experience with illness. We sensed we were living on borrowed time, which made us borrow as much time as possible, maxing out our credit lines, so to speak, until it was nearly too late.

And then, late this October, when Sam finally went in to be tested, his PSA had risen yet again, to a dangerously high 8.6. Again, he went for a biopsy, to Dr. Calagari, a urologist at Massachusetts General Hospital. And still we were in stunning denial about Sam's real condition. Embarrassing as it is to admit, we two highly capable researchers had not yet taken the trouble to learn that up to 50 percent of negative prostate cancer biopsies are in fact *false* negatives.

Calagari's phone call came late one autumn afternoon when the foliage was at its magnificent peak. I was in the bedroom folding laundry, keeping an eye on Isaac, now fifteen months, who was pushing a Matchbox car across the carpet. The telephone rang. Sam picked up on the downstairs extension. "Yes, Dr. Calagari. Hello."

I picked up the phone in the bedroom. Dr. Calagari's thin, reedy voice spoke slowly. "I'm afraid the biopsy came back positive. I'd get that gland out right away."

"Yes, well, thank you," said Sam. "For calling. One question, if I may. How many cores were cancerous?"

"Six," replied Calagari. "Out of nine. Means it's pretty aggressive. Gleason score of 7. Like I said, get rid of that gland."

Isaac ran his red car up the bed frame and across the spread. Then he let it go. Crash went the tiny toy.

So this was it, I thought. I felt strangely flat. I picked up my child and went downstairs, where Sam stood at the Mission desk in our front hall. Smiling.

"That's it," he said. "Now we know. Uncertainty's over."

"It's almost a relief, isn't it?" I said. "To finally know." For it's difficult to live in gray, and it takes a great effort to pretend that things are all right when really, deep down, you know they are not.

"We had a good run of things," says Sam, wistfully.

That was how we felt the first hour. I kept feeling I should feel something more dramatic. I should burst into tears; my face should turn china white. Mainly I was feeling hungry and thinking about whether black bean soup and brown bread and salad would be sufficient for dinner.

The second hour, Sam called a few people with his news. "The cancer's back," he announced. I couldn't help but hear a note of triumph in his voice. I couldn't quite place this note. Did he think he'd accomplished something? More likely, he knew he was calling with definitive news. Now we knew what we were up against. Our constant low-grade anxiety was about to end.

There's something else, too. I felt it the third hour, when I called my parents. Calling to announce a cancer diagnosis, you receive immediate and focused attention. All other news becomes secondary. A crisis has been set in motion, and this carries an air of excitement. Things are about to happen.

Perhaps this sense of change and motion made Sam and I giddy that first evening. He opened a bottle of wine he'd been saving, and this gave us an air, not of celebration, but of a marker having been reached. Of course, it was no surprise, we agreed. This is what we'd expected all along. The past year had been a giveaway. Now we were up against the real thing. Why hadn't Sam felt more urgency to get checked out sooner?

The answer, which we could only admit after two glasses of red Burgundy, was that we were not eager for Sam to have the messy salvage surgery. Yes, he'd been in denial. But the longer he put off surgery, the longer he'd retain a "normal" quality of life.

Waking, sober, the first morning after receiving the news, my head felt fuzzy. Saturday morning, frost on the windowpane, Isaac needs changing, have to call Mary to see if she wants to get together with the kids, and oh yes, Sam has cancer again. I felt a dull thud in the pit of my stomach, a new dull thud called dread, to which I was just getting accustomed and had not yet learned how to favor—much like the feeling when you've pulled a muscle and are still surprised by the discomfort, not yet having learned how to keep off the weight.

~~~~~~~~

We're really here, in Dr. Scardino's waiting room on the eleventh floor, where the sufferers are sedate. We're really here in New

York, and not at Baylor Medical in Houston, because during the past year Scardino left Houston to head the urology department at Memorial Sloan-Kettering. How convenient! How considerate! Less traveling for me! Sam joked at home. But there is no joking here in the waiting room; the tension is thick enough to cut with a scalpel. Men with graying hair read the *Wall Street Journal* through steel reading glasses. Or they sit; hands folded in their suited laps, tasseled loafer feet planted firmly on the carpet.

A nurse with her hair up in a clip calls Sam's name.

"Can my wife come too?" he asks.

"Not for the physical," she says. "After, to talk to the doctor."

Sam gathers up his coat and his black book bag, in which I saw him pack this morning *Complexity and Postmodernism*, *The Unreal Self*, and *The Mind and its Contents*. He will not read one word today.

He kisses me good-bye, his lips dry. Then he grimaces, and I see he is trying to make his DRE (digital rectal exam) into a joke. "Everyone wants a feel for himself," he says.

I smile, weakly. I press his palm, hard.

Midday, and the sun is strong. I sit before a row of windows and bask in the unexpected warmth.

Once again, Sam is rehearsing his death. In 1998, the popular books about prostate cancer maintain that there is no cure for recurrence after radiation. I see how Sam, preparing to die, draws back from fifteen-month-old Isaac, afraid to commit himself to a relationship he cannot promise to make good on. Other days, he wants to do everything for his son while there's still time.

"Let's not get ahead of ourselves," I say to him.

"I'm just trying to prepare for the inevitable."

I still don't believe Sam will die. But recently, once or twice, I've thought that *maybe* he will die. And then I've followed my sharp intake of breath, the dry sobs like knives, until I am able to ask myself: Of what am I most afraid? Of missing him, for sure: his hearty voice in the morning, the blustery way he enters a room. A particular person with whom I have such a long and intimate history. But I am most afraid of having to explain his absence to Isaac. And then I peer far down, as if into a ravine, and I tell myself that I could, if I had to, raise our son alone. Plenty of women do. And then, somehow, I am able to detach from my situation just a tiny bit and, as the Buddhists teach, let go. I am less hysterical now.

I follow the nurse down a long hallway, at the end of which I find my husband.

We walk into a tiny, cluttered office. A handsome, tall man with reddish hair and a movie-star cleft in his chin dominates the space. Dr. Peter Scardino. At first glance he reminds me of the guy in high school who won every award and had friends in every clique. Our surgeon-to-be extends his hand in greeting. This is the hand of one of the few men in the world who can perform the challenging salvage radical prostectomy. The hand of the man voted one of the best doctors in the United States, a stellar entry in *Who's Who*. I expect such a hand to be, at the very least, like one belonging to a master pianist: strong, flexible, and distinguished. I expect a glow around the thumb, or better yet, an extra finger; some sign that he can cut away my husband's malignancy.

But the hand that Dr. Scardino offers is quite ordinary. Neither small nor large, scrubbed pink, with three freckles above the thumb. We shake heartily.

"Pleased to meet you," he says.

We take our seats, ceremoniously.

"We have questions," I say.

Scardino nods. Of course.

From his pocket Sam pulls a folded piece of yellow lined

paper. The paper rustles loudly. As the designated note taker, I open my spiral notebook.

Haltingly, Sam reads. "What are my chances at survival?"

Scardino leans forward, presses his fingers together in a pyramid. "If the margins are clear, as I expect they will be, you have a reasonably good chance at survival beyond five years."

"Beyond five years?" I ask, my voice rising with incredulity. Five years is not enough, I think. In five years Isaac will be only seven.

The doctor explains that survival beyond five years generally means that the patient is out of danger.

"You said 'reasonably good chance,'" says Sam. "Could you be more specific?"

As an answer, Scardino pushes a piece of paper across the desk. On the paper is a graph. RATE OF CURE read the large letters across the top. Running down the left side of the graph: PSA AT TIME OF SURGERY—TUMOR STAGING—GLEASON SCORE.

Scardino runs his finger across the graph. "Let's see now," he murmurs. "With a PSA of 8 . . ."

But Sam is figuring, calculating—I can feel his brain on fire. "Seventy-eight percent," he exclaims, triumphant as a game show contestant with the right answer. "I'd say that's damn reasonable."

In the best of circumstances, I am slow to comprehend graphs. But here, on the eleventh floor of Sloan-Kettering, I need everything confirmed. "You mean there's a seventy-eight percent chance of being cured!"

"Seventy-eight percent chance at living out a normal lifespan," says Sam. "Unless I get hit by a truck," he adds.

"Isn't that so much better . . ." I begin.

"Than we'd hoped for," Sam finishes.

I feel the blood surge to my heart, my cold hands. I write in my notebook: "78% rate of cure." Across the desk from us, Scardino looks satisfyingly full around the jowls.

Sam takes a deep breath. "What about the complications?"

Scardino's hands move as gracefully as birds taking flight. He sketches possible future scenarios. He won't make any promises, he says—he is too sophisticated to guarantee that Sam's future will be entirely complication-free—but he exudes something even more compelling than optimism: confidence. Confidence in his surgical abilities, and confidence in Sam's and my courage to take a balanced look at our possible futures. "Two out of four men," Scardino explains, "will recover continence entirely within a year. One out of four men will have mild leakage throughout the day. Nothing you can't live with. One out of four men will have chronic problems."

We nod soberly. Of course there are risks. We've done our research. We understand.

Sam forges ahead with question number three: "What about sexual functioning?"

Scardino swallows, his Adam's apple dipping. This is the hard-sell part of the consult, the not-so-fine print that can break the deal. "Viagra," he says, his voice smooth as a fine cognac, "is not particularly effective after a salvage. We have various options. Penile injections usually work. If necessary, a penile implant can be done."

Unlike the other specialists we've seen, Scardino includes me with plenty of eye contact. He is the first urologist to make me feel not merely like a wifely appendage but like a participant. "This is about my husband," I want to signal back with my eyes. "I'm just here to take notes." But a warning light in the surgeon's gold-flecked pupils warns that I do not yet fathom what lies ahead.

"Also," he says, brightening with glee, "I can sometimes graft a nerve from the foot onto the penis. It can take up to two years for things to take, but partial erections are then possible. Viagra can take you the rest of the way."

"Can I coauthor the paper?" jokes Sam.

Good, I think. Sam is joking. Good, I think. We have found a way forward. For so long we have lived in helpless fear, and now, mixed with the euphoria of learning that Sam's chance of survival is good, I feel tremendous relief. We can act.

"Sexual functioning," says Sam. "Incontinence," says his new surgeon. Do they hear the sharp blade behind those words? For we don't know what we're saying, none of us do. We have no idea of the bargain we strike.

Out on the street it is a chilly day in Manhattan. I look at my watch: three o'clock. I turn to Sam, see his face more relaxed than in months and months. "We still have time," I say. "We're in New York! We have a babysitter!"

"Let's walk," Sam says. "It's a good day to walk."

We button up against the cold. "I need a coat," he says. It's true, he's still wearing the olive green raincoat he wore to our first date so many years ago.

"Barney's," I say.

And so we fall into step walking across town on 67th Street and left on Madison. We share the sidewalk with brisk holiday shoppers, all intent on their goals, and all preoccupied with concerns so very different from ours—Sam's health. Passing shop windows decorated in red ribbon and gold glitter, I can pretend for a moment that we are in New York on a holiday getaway. We walk and walk, mittened hand in hand, our breath spiraling white and pure.

Inside the department store the sweet-scented rooms sparkle as if there is no such thing as pain or death. Up and up we ride the gold-leaf elevator. In the Men's Department a salesman loses no time sizing up Sam; his careful, measured glance takes in nearly as much information as the surgeon's statistical records. Once again I am a bystander, a witness to a specialized men's world, the world my son will inherit. Whereas the doctor studies Sam's cellular troubles, this salesman is in charge of appearances. "I've got something for you," he finally says. "Wait right here."

He disappears deep into the racks and then reappears holding up a blue wool coat. "Try this."

Raglan sleeves, generous cut, soft drape. . . . When Sam slips on the coat he looks bright and new and handsome. He looks like a man with a definite future. If I met you today, I think, I'd go out with you in a heartbeat.

"Looks good," says our man. "Classic style, top quality. A coat like this can last you the rest of your life."

Sam's eyes, suddenly fragile, meet mine. *The rest of your life.* I see him study the white slip of a price tag, see him calculate how many years he will have to live for this coat to make prudent economic sense. It is no bargain. I see now how things will be. On the outside my husband will be sharp and good-looking, a man able to continue in the world. He will stay warm. But on the inside? He will be cut and stitched, he will bleed and scar. Bitter fluids will drip into his veins, and each new step will be a trial.

And what about me? I will be privy to the scars and bleedings. My happiness with Sam will be forever tempered to bitter-sweet. I will grow older. I will come to terms with my life.

At home, Sam sits at the kitchen table, a neat Glenfiddich before him. "I'm never going to get it up again after the surgery." He speaks evenly, just delivering the facts.

"Scardino didn't say that exactly," I say. I am standing at the sink, letting the water run hot, the supper dishes stacked and waiting.

"Yeah, but that's what he implied," says Sam. "We have to prepare ourselves for the end of sex."

"We'll cuddle and get a vibrator," I say. "Besides, sex is about a lot more than just erections. We'll eat good food. We'll enjoy our son."

Sam taps the side of his scotch glass. "You'll take a lover," he says. I can't tell if he's accusing or predicting. "Just don't let me know about them," he mutters, then tosses the amber liquid down his throat.

"Affairs," I say, drawing the word out. "I'm not that kind of woman." Which is true. I'm the loyal and steadfast kind of woman, a tolerant one who values trust, confidentiality. But I'm also a sensual woman, and one who values passion. "I don't know," I say to Sam. I turn to him, hands on my hips. "I don't *want* one. I don't want to lose the closeness with you."

And then, because this line of thinking is too difficult for me to even contemplate right now, I flippantly add: "Besides, I don't have anyone in mind."

The lines of his face fall in grateful response.

"But how do you *feel?*" he asks. "Sit down. Have a drink. We need to talk about this."

"I don't feel much of anything," I say. Which is also true. To please him, I sit down in his offered chair.

"Drink?" he offers.

"No, thanks."

"How do *you* feel about losing your sexual partner?" he insists. "About saying good-bye to your sex life?"

"I just don't know what to feel," I tell him. "I'm not thinking about it. I'm numb, I guess. Maybe you thinking about it so much makes me not have to. I'm concentrating on the surgery. The end of sex? That's the bargain, right? Your sex or your life."

I can see that Sam is not convinced. I so very much want him to go into this surgery without any nagging misgivings. "I've changed my mind," I say. "I'll have that drink."

Sam pours out the scotch, hands me the glass, and raises his own. "To us," he says.

His eyes are trusting and scared. "To us," I repeat. I tip my head back.

"Anyway, who says we're all that different from other married couples?" I continue. "Exactly who is having such great sex? No one I know."

"Don't expect me to believe that you really believe that," says Sam. "Don't underestimate what's going to happen to us."

I take another burning sip. "I've had enough sex," I say. "Besides, doesn't every couple strike some kind of a bargain?" I start listing couples we know. Mag makes more of the money, Joe takes more care of the kids. Abby gave up an outdoorsy life when she married urbanite Philip. "And Eugene? You know what he told me? That he always wanted a child, but Sharon chose not to."

Sam raises a hand in protest. "Okay, enough. It's just that I'm not too thrilled about them cutting off my dick."

"You know that's not what's going to happen."

"Maybe it's not worth it," he says. "Such a compromised life."

"You can't get it up if you're dead," I say.

"Who says life is so great?"

"We have a kid," I say, "who needs his Dad."

We are home from a Chanukah party. Since Isaac was born, we don't see much of Sam's old gang, but we went to the party tonight to break the news of Sam's impending operation. Miranda said, "Let me know what I can do. Really, I mean it." Willy said, "I'll be calling you, pal, on a regular basis now."

I saw Sam come to life again with the sympathy and attention. People cared. Sam ate and drank. He talked and talked, proud to be an expert on his own disease.

At home, the sheets are cool and clean. Sam is warm, his legs sinewy. I snuggle up. "Did you remember to turn down the thermostat?" I ask.

"Yep. Mailed the stack of bills, too," he says.

"Isaac fed Misha Bear pieces of toast and egg this morning," I tell him. "So adorable."

His hand traces a line along my hip. "Have you seen how he scoots down the stairs headfirst?"

"Fearless," I say. I move my thigh closer. "We should try to keep him that way."

"Did he have a nap?"

With light insistence, his hand travels down my thigh. "Did you call Mary back?"

"Let's talk later," I murmur.

His mouth tastes of raisin-spiced wine. He is food, he is drink, and I must nourish myself upon his plush belly.

He pulls me up so to that we are lying eye to eye. In the muted light he looks twenty years younger, a young man just starting out: new wife, new baby, new house. I haven't seen much of this person lately. During daytime hours Sam often impersonates a washed-up, embittered man who is prematurely entering old age.

I open to this new man's touch. I climb on top of him and I widen until I understand at last that I am made to be filled and replenished. We know each other, Sam and I, as a fantastic flying creature, and we scale great heights.

Sam and I talked to many people during this interim between diagnosis and surgery, and I discovered that people display quite a range of responses toward serious illness.

An old friend from childhood is home for the holidays from the West Coast, visiting her parents. She calls, as she always does when in town, and we catch up on the news. I hear about her new job and the various activities of her kids before interrupting with: "Sam has prostate cancer. He's going in for surgery next month."

"This is a really bad week!" exclaims this friend since third grade. "I just got off the phone with Michael and his newborn is in ICU, they don't know if she's going to make it. And Mandy Oppenheimer, who lives across the street from my parents, just came home from open-heart surgery. I can't believe how bad it is!"

I put down the phone and let her continue in this vein for as long as she needs. Unfortunately, I say at the conversation's end, I do not think I'll be able to see her this visit.

An acquaintance I run into at the supermarket, her cart laden with fresh navel oranges and soy products, is equally stinging. "You have to think positively!" she practically shouts over the pasta bin. "Imagery can be so powerful! And make sure to write out an affirmative statement for your surgeon."

"An affirmative what?" I say.

"You write out a message for the surgeon to repeat when Sam is under anesthesia. Something like, 'You will heal easily and completely and be restored to wholeness.'"

"Okay," I say, backing my cart down the cereal aisle. "I'll mention it to Sam."

But the person who most disappoints me in her attempt to help is a therapist I seek out specifically for support in my crisis.

I am referred to this particular woman because she herself has recently lost her husband to a long disease. Perhaps we do not get off on the right footing, because at our first session I blurt: "I don't want to be like you! I don't want my husband to die!"

I don't mean to imply anything more than what these words assert, but in a therapeutic setting, where I sit in a black leather chair across from a gray-haired woman old enough to be my mother, my statement carries more weight than I intended. That becomes one of our sticking points: I want to speak about the literal, here-and-now crisis, how to cope on a day-to-day basis, and she, I feel, wants to dig into the crevices of my psyche. When I want to cut back our sessions to every other week because time feels so precious just now—I have to choose between therapy and being pampered at the salon, which, to tell the truth, often feels like a better use of the money than talking about, for example, the birthday parties I wasn't invited to at age eight—the therapist wants to spend three sessions talking about my resistance and need for control.

In the end, I march myself to the mental health department at my HMO and ask to see a psychopharmacologist. She spends half an hour asking me a series of serious questions: Do you often feel you cannot cope? *Yes.* Are you crying a lot? *Yes.* Having trouble sleeping? *Yes.* She writes me out a prescription for Zoloft. Within a week of taking the antidepressant, I have acquired the sense that an air cushion surrounds my body, one that allows me to feed my child and talk to my husband without bursting into tears. Under my breath I curse the therapist who did not offer me the solace her profession provides.

I do not mean to imply that other people cannot help. Amy, a close friend since high school who is now a doctor, takes the time to confer with Sam and me on the phone. She refers us to a urologist colleague. We report to her after each consult, sounding out our responses and opinions. In general, people who have lived through a serious illness themselves, either as patient or caretaker, are the most forthright and useful. They are honest about the challenges we will face. One friend survived brain cancer ten years previous. I took courage from his wife's advice: "In every moment, no matter how difficult, I just kept asking myself, 'What can I do right now to help things? What action can I take?' When he first came home from the hospital and was frightened to sleep alone and I knew I needed my sleep, I moved in a cot so that our son could take some of the nights. When one doctor told us it was a hopeless case, I sought out more opinions until I found someone who had a solution."

Ultimately, though, I am alone with all this. And I turn to

words, as I have for most of my life. Ever since that moment of washing my face in the ladies room in Arpege and realizing that there was no one to whom I could turn for consolation, I have been writing things down. I open my laptop and spew. I record Isaac's milestones—first smile, first time sleeping through the night—but mostly I write out, in leaden prose, my terror. I cling to the idea that by writing things down I can alleviate my pain. I dream that in the future I can shape my experience artfully enough so that another person will read my words and garner some comfort.

January 19, the date of Sam's surgery, approaches. We make preparations. Isaac will stay with my parents; Rita will babysit extra hours. Will our child be damaged without us for a week? "He'll be fine," our pediatrician assures. "Take care of yourselves."

We investigate postoperative care. A former patient of Scardino's with whom Sam speaks on the phone says he slept in a reclining chair after coming home from the hospital. Should we buy a recliner? Install safety bars in the shower stall? Stock up on incontinence supplies? In the end, we do none of these. Instead, Sam borrows a digital camcorder.

"For posterity," he says. "For Isaac in case I die."

"Will you stop being morbid," I say. "You're not going to die. I won't let you. Scardino won't let you."

"Never can tell what will happen on the operating table," Sam replies. "Besides, it's never going to be the same after this. A *part* of me is going to die."

Fifteen-months-old Isaac takes his first wobbly steps, and Sam films his unsteady path across the carpet. Isaac hits the metal pot with a wooden spoon; I put my hands on my ears in mock horror. A long strip of light on the gray carpet. The floor-to-ceiling bookshelves. Sam sitting in our Tyrolean antler chair, grim-faced, stuttering to tell Isaac how much he loves him.

I can't stand the weightiness of each moment. I hate looking at our ordinary domestic scenes against a backdrop of tragedy. Also, my inner resources are sorely strained with the need to be the optimistic one, the positive-thinking one, the practical one.

The temperature's dropping and the nights are long and cold. The week before Sam's operation, I find myself going to sleep earlier and earlier, the better to reserve my strength and blot out the terror. Sam, however, is rightly terrified, and his way is to stay up later and later, unable to sleep. He's going over bills, surfing obscure sites on the Net, playing solitaire with his computer. One A.M., two A.M., three A.M. I hear him come to bed. Sometimes I don't wake at all, for I am at the bottom-most echelon on the ladder of sleep, the one closest to amphibian. On one of those nights I am pulled from sleep. The bedroom is steamy with heat. There's a smell like leaves burning. The overhead light glares like a prisoner's cell. My mouth is terribly parched. And what's that clanging?

I sit up in bed and throw off the down comforter, under which I am sweating. "What the hell is going on?" I yell.

Sam is wearing nothing but a thin T-shirt. "I've found a way to trick the furnace," he says, smiling. "By closing off the downstairs vents."

"What?" I am disoriented, annoyed at being woken by a mad plumber. Oh, yes, I remember now, our dysfunctional heating system that never warms the upstairs rooms. We've been complaining that the pipes don't work.

"The thermostat reads way down when I turn off the vents

that way, and the furnace is tricked into pumping and pumping." His eyes are glowing with success.

"What's with the *noise?*" It's not an alarm, I realize, but the radiator.

"Water in the pipes. Can you feel how warm it is up here?"

"It's hot as hell!" I yell. "Ninety degrees! Are you crazy? What do you think you're doing? We don't need it hot like this."

Now his mouth turns down, a wee bit chastised by my scolding. "Yeah, I guess maybe I overdid it," he admits.

My tongue is thick inside my pasty mouth, and now I have lost it. "Could you at least get me a glass of water? Do you realize how much I've been doing for you lately, letting you feel whatever it is you need to feel, do whatever it is you need to do, making no demands, taking care of everything myself? Don't you know how terrified I am too? I hate being the strong one all the time. And now, look what you've done. Don't go crazy on me, please. You've proved your point. Turn down the heat. And do you think you could manage a glass of water?"

I am hyperventilating. I am crazed myself. By the way his eyes narrow I can see I have scared Sam. Without saying a word, he walks out of the room. I am shaking when he returns with a clear glass tumbler. He holds it out to me and watches me while I drink.

January 18, the day before Sam's operation, he and I arrive at Logan Airport, hurrying, late, our bags flapping awkwardly against our legs, only to hear a voice on the speaker system announce that LaGuardia is shut down in a snowstorm, our flight postponed.

It's four P.M. Check-in at the hospital is tomorrow morning at nine o'clock. If we don't make it to New York tonight, the operation will be cancelled. And the cancer cells are dividing more quickly now. And we're prepared for this operation. We *want* it now.

Snowflakes as delicate as doilies are swirling outside the airport window. When did snow become our adversary? Nature our opponent? Because it is nature that instructs the cancer cells to divide and multiply until Sam is fit carrion for the grave.

We will not follow nature. We will fight nature. We will make it through this snowstorm; we will get past this disease. We are bound for the grand operating theater of modern medicine.

Sam calls up Amtrak. There is a train leaving for New York City in 27 minutes.

We hail a cab and speed to South Station. We stand in line to buy our tickets. We check nothing. "All aboard," shouts the conductor.

Single file in the narrow corridor, we carry our luggage to our sleeping compartment. This is our brainstorm; we will travel with a private toilet so that Sam can use the prescribed pre-op laxative. Two bunks, a tiny sink, and a tiny television set also make up our quarters.

Sam checks his watch. "Eight o'clock. I just made it. I have to start the GoLytely immediately." He mixes pink powder with water into the bottom of a plastic jug. He takes a swig, screws up his mouth in disgust. "Vile," he pronounces it. "Absolutely vile."

On the top bunk I lie on my red blanket, bury my head in a pillow. Much later Sam will tell me this trip is the comic high point of his disease. "Write it so it's funny," he'll say. "I sat on the pot and watched *Zorro* and *Toy Story* on a tiny TV. With the sound *off*, while drinking GoLytely and exercising my sphincter muscles." And then he'll emit a gruff laugh. "What a trip from hell."

But I slip into a twilight sleep, where I pray, into the darkness outside the minute square of a window, that Sam can empty himself in a spiritual sense. I pray he can find his own way back to health. I pray that we will come through this. Chug chug chug sounds my beloved train. When I was twenty-two I took a train across Canada and then a ferryboat up the fjords to Alaska. I was visiting Tokiko. Summer, and the sun shone fiery red until midnight, when she and I danced with New Jersey boys turned mountain men, an old-timey band stomping out reels on the makeshift stage. I was a girl then, and when I arched my back against my partner's arm and spun around and around, my long hair fanning out, the room was a kaleidoscope of joy. Chug chug sounds the train. That was long ago. Chug chug. Where are you going now? Chug chug. My eyes close, mercifully.

It's two in the morning when the Twilight Shoreliner pulls into Penn Station. The street is frigid with bone-chilling cold. No one is out. Shoulder to shoulder stand Sam and I—two shuddering figures in long coats. And then, at last, a yellow taxi comes into view. ✦

FROM BURGUNDY
TO CHARDONNAY

I spend the five hours of Sam's surgery in the Family Waiting Area, a large sun-drenched sitting room that overlooks a garden. Ordinarily I love being alone, and since Isaac was born and Sam got sick, I crave solitude. I'd actually thought today would be a time for myself. Little did I know the extreme vigilance that accompanies waiting for a loved one while he's on the operating table. Enviously, I look over at the six Hispanic sisters, each one dark-eyed and beautiful, dressed in heels and tailored suits; as a group they are continually whispering, stroking, or embracing. I watch with envy, too, the extended Indian family camped out in one corner: the little children asleep on older siblings' laps, mothers unpacking sweets from coolers, the men chattering into cell phones.

I wish now I'd accepted Cousin Arleen's offer to come up from Florida and sit with me. Alone, I sip my stale coffee. I pull my knees up to my chest. I check my watch with the large wall clock. I'm beyond worry—I'm in a heightened, out-of-time, out-of-body state where I need no food, no drink, and no sleep.

"Vigil" is the word that comes again and again to mind. Under ordinary circumstances, I am not a religious person, but this vigil feels like one that should be accompanied by candles and prayer. I get up from my seat, once, to tour the gift shop immediately adjacent, where I am inexplicably drawn to the quaintly decorated plaques. JESUS LOVES ME. GIVE ME THE STRENGTH TO ACCEPT WHAT I CANNOT CHANGE. THE LORD WORKS IN MYSTERIOUS WAYS. Faith is what's needed while one's beloved is cut open, his blood draining while the disease is rooted out. Faith is about all that can be exercised for the hours that Sam hovers in twilight sleep. For Sam is crossing a country now, I sense, under the blankness of anesthesia, his soul floating above the operating table.

I dare not leave the Family Waiting Area, ostensibly because it is to this location that the O.R. nurse will report, midway through Sam's operation, that although he's lost a lot of blood, my husband is doing well, and the doctors are getting ready to stitch him back up. But the real reason neither I nor any of the waiting families can leave this blessedly lit room is because, as in a church or temple or mosque, our collective prayer has made it a sacred space, one I dare not leave for the strength it gives me to hold steadfast.

When Dr. Scardino finally comes for me, the picture window is already darkened with winter evening. In clogs and green surgical scrubs, he is even taller than I remembered. He ushers me into a conference room.

"I am very pleased with the operation," he says. "Technically, that is."

I dare not breathe.

The first thing that Scardino tells me is that the nerve bundles controlling erections were very thick, and so he was able to spare about half the nerves. "That bodes well," Scardino says, his voice kind, "for at least partial functioning. And then med—"

"Viagra," I say, too hurriedly, not quite understanding why my husband's surgeon has begun his debriefing with the potency report.

"Viagra, presumably," says Scardino, "could take you the rest of the way."

I do not yet see how he sees me. Relative to other wives of prostate cancer sufferers, I am a young one, and recently married. Things are going to be difficult for me in a way they are not for a woman married fifty years, one whose greatest pleasure now is being with her grandchildren.

Scardino describes Sam's lymph nodes, rectum, and seminal vesicles. "Fine, fine, fine," he says. And the margins look clear, which is very good news because that means the cancer has most likely not spread beyond the gland.

"You know his PSA was up to 12 before he went in?" he asks.

I nod. Sam was beside himself with this knowledge.

"With a number that high," Scardino cautions, "we have to be concerned until we get the pathology report. But, in general, I am very pleased."

He stands up. Our meeting is over. I want to say something that lets him know I appreciate his surgical art, and understand the fine points of prostate disease, but instead, like a supplicant, I grab his hand and cry out, "Thank you, thank you, thank you."

I am so grateful that Sam is alive and the operation is over, that when I see Sam, strapped to a hospital bed set at a sharp vertical angle, as if on a macabre carnival ride, breathing into a clear plastic mask, his eyelids yellow-tinged and his arm bruised purple, I am graced with the deepest tenderness for this man, my husband.

The next morning I ride the elevator up to the eighth floor, to Genital Urological Surgery, where I find my husband in excellent spirits. He is sitting up in bed, talking to a nurse. When he sees me, he waves his arms in greeting. He kisses me on the lips. "I'm alive! I'm here! Scardino got it all out!"

He looks like a giant octopus, with tubes sprouting from his arms. He shows me the self-regulating button on his morphine pump. His hair, flying wildly in all directions, here in a cancer shop, where bald heads abound, makes him appear especially lucky.

He shows me his catheter tube, which pokes out from under the blankets and feeds into a plastic bag the size of a child's balloon. He explains that the flowing red liquid, urine mixed with blood, is the color of Burgundy. "The doctors say I can go home when it turns the color of Chardonnay."

He turns to the nurse, who stands to one side. "Of course, no one's mentioned what vintage."

The nurse is very young, her sunshine hair pulled back in a ponytail. "This is Serena," says my husband. "She's about to change my scrotum pad."

Serena smiles perfunctorily at me, the superfluous wife. "Excuse us," she says, and pulls the curtain closed around Sam's bed.

This first day after the operation is a busy one. I hardly have time to visit with my husband, who has been literally taken from me and handed over to the nurses and hospital infrastructure.

Sam receives visits from the Pain Team—a man and a woman, both very serious and dressed in brown pantsuits—who monitor Sam's morphine; from the Vein Lady, a large, laughing woman with gleaming teeth who checks the IV tubes; and from Scardino's postdoctoral fellows, who huddle around Sam to peer and poke, conferring with one another as they study Sam, their medical specimen. Sam lies in bed like some head of state, euphoric with painkillers and attention.

I ride the elevator down to the second floor. I am lost. I follow the wrong arrows, I misread signs. At long last I reach the hospital cafeteria and load up my tray with weak coffee and runny eggs. "Visitor or staff?" queries the cashier.

"Just visiting," I reply.

When I sit down at a long table, I realize just how numb are my arms and legs. My back aches. My brain is cotton. There is nothing for me to do for Sam. Am I jealous of the sudden intimacy sprung up between Sam the patient and his young nurses? Sweetie, he called the one with the ponytail. On the Genital Urological ward, where almost all the patients are older men, the nurses are noticeably young and sweet—daughterly—as they administer to their injured charges. Silly for me to be jealous, I decide, when the nurses brighten and care. Still, I feel helpless. I am disconnected from Sam. Who is he now that his body is forever changed? Who am I? All I can say for now is that he and I are undergoing a seismic shift in our relations, and I am struggling to keep my balance.

When I return, Sam is sitting up in bed, waving a piece of paper. "The pathology report! The margins came back clear!"

This is the best news we can receive. I breathe huge sighs of relief, realizing only now what an effort it's taken to buoy myself up. That the margins came back clear means we can hope for a normal lifespan for Sam.

125

"You must be exhausted," he says to me, sitting slumped in the visitor's chair. "I'm fine here. Go take a nap or something. You don't need to be here all the time."

Back at Helmsley Medical Towers, where the desk clerk is forever asleep at the desk and where the lobby smells perpetually of ammonia, I ride a slow elevator up to my room. I want to sleep, and in the worst way, but the telephone is ringing. As wife and as witness, I have many calls to answer, and many calls to take. He is fine; I am fine, I say again and again. The margins were clear. They got it all out. How is Isaac? Give him a kiss. I miss him.

And then, finally, I fall into a restless doze. Sirens are screaming past outside. Down the street, in the rooms of Sloan-Kettering, people are dying; but for now, Sam will not. Behind my closed eyelids is a rainbow, with colors I haven't seen since I was a child. I fall into magenta; I fall into aquamarine; I fall into plum. My eyelids will not cease fluttering, and my teeth, I realize with surprise, are clenched shut.

Opiates sustain Sam for two days. Then, the brown-suited Pain Team is back at his bedside. "Time to down your dose," they announce in unison. "Tomorrow—Percoset pills."

Sam takes this as good news. He is making progress. No more dry mouth from the morphine. But I am a little worried. Who will Sam be now?

The next day, I know.

"Lower the blind, will you?" Sam says to me, irritated and short-fused. "The light's in my eyes."

There's something wrong with his leg; he cannot walk.

During surgery, Scardino was forced to cut a leg nerve. This is not usual procedure, but a complication due to the radiation scarring from six years ago. A plastic surgeon immediately grafted the nerve back together, but it will take time to for it to regenerate. Problem is, walking is supposed to speed Sam's healing. Sam is worried now, about when he will walk again. Bedridden, the tiny paper cups that contain his pain pills are within reach, as are glasses, water, and newspaper. His urine still flows burgundy red into the catheter. I go over to the window, where bright bouquets from friends back in Boston line the sill. I pull the blind all the way down.

"Not that far. It makes me claustrophobic," Sam snaps. "A little higher."

It's the hostility in his voice that unnerves me. "Please," I say, in more of a whine than I'd intended. "I'm trying to help." Then I fiddle clumsily with the cord.

"It's a simple window shade," Sam yells. "What's wrong?"

What's wrong is the Hasidic black hats I passed on my way to Sam's room just now, the men standing in the hall conferring in low tones, the women crying into handkerchiefs, the nurses inside the empty room, stripping the bedsheets. What's wrong is the bald teenager in the wheelchair, his terror-filled eyes darting feverishly. What's wrong is my husband. Why is his scrotum blown up as big as a grapefruit? His belly has an oozing cut held together by staples. His penis sprouts a plastic tube; he is pissing blood.

I bow my head, put my face in my hands so Sam will not see the tears. "Sorry," he says. "For being short with you. The pain makes me irritable."

"It's just that . . ." I stammer, "it's hard to see you like this."

"One day at a time," he says. "The operation was a success. Now we'll see if the patient will live."

I do not laugh. "Could you try again with the blind?" he says. I can hear the effort it takes for him to be patient. "It *is* a little dark in here."

That evening, the real pain hits. Sam is racked with cramps and spasms. The catheter tube is empty of liquid. It's after nine, and a skeletal night crew staffs the floor. "Let me finish here, dear," mumbles the matronly form of a nurse when I find her in another patient's room, bent over the bed.

"But my husband's in terrible pain!"

She nods, unperturbed. "They get that way."

"But there's nothing draining in the catheter!"

Her eyes are swollen bags. "I'll be there as soon as I can, dear."

I huff back to Sam. "The nurse will be here soon," I tell him.

"I can't wait!" shouts Sam. His face is colorless, his hair plastered to his head in sweat. He presses the intercom button. "Nurse! Nurse, please." We wait five minutes, ten minutes. Sam is moaning, delirious; I'm afraid he will lose consciousness. He presses the intercom. "Murderers!" he bellows into all the rooms of the eighth floor. "Murderers, all of you!"

Finally, a nurse arrives. Not the matron but a beanpole blonde. She checks Sam's meds, his pulse, his temperature, and then shrugs her shoulders. Nothing appears to be wrong. "I'd like you to page the doctor on call," I say, surprised at my assertiveness.

When the doctor finally arrives, he is Iranian and heavyset. He looks at the catheter tubing, empty and clear of liquid. He listens when Sam describes the painful spasms. "Blockage problem is what it sounds like," the doctor declares. "I'll have to irrigate your bladder."

He fills a basin with saline solution, then fills what looks like a large needle or turkey baster with the solution. Detaches the catheter's tube from the overnight bag; attaches the baster to the catheter. He then pumps water up the catheter and into the bladder. This is supposed to wash back any blood clots caught in the bladder neck.

I see Sam grimace in pain as the pressure on the bladder builds. The doctor sets the basin on the bed, pulls back on the needle plunger and detaches the needle. Water and urine start draining into the basin. After a few seconds, something resembling a cherry pit falls into the basin. "That," says the doctor, pointing his finger, "was the cause of your trouble. A blood clot." He shakes his head.

"It's as bad as labor," he says to me.

Having birthed a tiny pit, one that will never ripen into fruit but one that, perhaps, signals a new life ahead, Sam can rest. I see his eyes close. His breath comes easy now. I stay until the color returns to his face.

The phone wakes me from a deep sleep. I start to bolt from bed, confused, thinking Isaac is in danger, but then I remember where I am: New York. Hemsley Medical Towers. I reach for the phone.

"I'm here," says a familiar male voice. "How is he? By the way, hello."

It's Sam's brother Alan, flown in from Tel Aviv.

"You woke me up," I say. "Where are you?"

"Two floors down." He laughs. "So—how is he?"

I brief Alan about the pathology report, the blood clot. "He's getting pretty difficult," I say. "Yelling at the nurses, and—"

"A genetic trait," Alan interrupts. "When the going gets tough, we get mean as hell."

"I guess I'm just getting to know the family," I say.

"Meet me downstairs?" says Alan. "I'd rather go over there together, this first time."

Sam and Alan are not close. When I met Alan, one of the first things he said to me was, "Sam and I have the same mother and the same father but we're not brothers." This was three years ago, shortly after Mildred's funeral. We were emptying her Skokie apartment—a Herculean task—which she lived in during the summer months, when Palm Springs was unbearably hot. What kept the brothers apart? Differing views on Israeli politics—Sam an early peacemonger, Alan a career army officer—sibling rivalries, Alan raising three kids on the kibbutz, Sam pursuing a doctoral degree in Cambridge.

Hurriedly now, I wash and dress and take the elevator down to the dim lobby. Alan is bulky where Sam is compact, formally dressed while Sam is casual, and balding where Sam's hair flourishes. Right now, his left leg twitches with impatience. He kisses me on the cheek. "Ready? Let's go. I didn't bring the right clothes, though. Look . . ." he motions to his tan trenchcoat. "This is the warmest thing I brought."

Out on York Avenue, the vendors are hawking coffee from silver carts.

"You want one?" asks Alan. "I'm buying."

I warm my bare hands on the paper cup and breathe in wisps of steam. I tell Alan, "I'm pretty much exhausted by the whole thing. I'm not cut out for this line of work." I bend to the bitter liquid too quickly and it burns my lip. I turn my face away, not wanting him to see my pain.

"I'm here now," says Alan. "We can take turns staying with him. You can have some time off."

I watch my brother-in-law as we get off the elevator to Sam's floor. As always, I brace myself for the sight of the men taking their daily walk around the ward. Skinny silhouettes like something out of Giacometti, they list to one side, pulling tall metal IV poles.

"I was in the army," Alan says, as if in response to my fear. "I've seen death before."

In Sam's room, the brothers attempt a hug, but it ends up as more of a pat. "Thanks for coming," says Sam.

"You think I have so many brothers I can spare one?"

Sam says, "It looks like I'm going to live. As to the quality of my life, that remains to be seen. It's like the joke where the two women are eating in a restaurant in the Catskills. One complains to the other, 'The food here is terrible.' And her friend replies—"

"Yes, and the portions are so small," Alan finishes.

They know the same jokes. What's more, they still laugh at them. That must count for something, I think.

Now that Alan is here, I don't have to carry everything myself. I can share the worry. His humor helps to sustain us. Tonight, the joke is that Alan and I will dine out, but that we are forcing ourselves to do so only as a charitable gesture to Sam, who cannot even finish a bowl of Jell-O.

We go to the Union Square Cafe, because that is where Sam wants to go. When the waiter brings the bread and water and wine, I realize that it's the first real food I've eaten in days. I chew slowly, wooing my taste buds back to life, draining my glass. The room is filled with well-dressed people having a good time—a world I've almost forgotten. Alan sits opposite me. Over the main course we talk about movies, his kids, Isaac, the camera lens for which he's shopping, and the recent vacation he and his girlfriend took to Greece. It doesn't matter what we say, really, so long as we don't talk about the hospital. When the dessert menu arrives and Alan sees me hesitate, he says, "Come on. Force yourself. Remember, we're doing this for Sam."

After dinner, Alan and I stop by the hospital to check on Sam. We find him writhing in pain, holding on to his belly. "It's the blood clot again," he moans. "Except the nurse won't page a doctor."

I am out in the hall in a fury. Where are the nurses? I am seasoned now, no longer fearful, ready to fight. I stride to the nurses' station. "What's this about not calling a doctor for my husband?" I yell. "He needs to have his bladder irrigated. He needs to have his . . ."

"Honey, just settle down. We've ordered some more medication."

"That's not the problem," I shout. "You need to page the doctor. Right now."

"I'll let my supervisor know," she says. The way she looks at me lets me know I am no longer a supplicant in this hospital, but someone to contend with—one of the difficult wives.

I go back to Sam's room. "The doctor's on his way," I say confidently. "I can't believe this is happening again."

Alan is standing in the middle of the room, his leg twitching. Sam has his hand over his eyes. "This is just like Andrea," he says. He is practically sobbing, as if trying to pass a clot in his heart as well as his bladder. "She shrieked for six hours and no one bothered to help. Botched liver biopsy. She bled to death." He repeats himself. *"Bled to death.* This is how it happens."

"Don't think about Andrea," I snap. This is too much, coping with his first wife's illness right now. "She was much weaker than you are now. Don't compare yourself to her."

But Alan shoots me a look. He motions for me to lower my

voice. I am shouting now. I resent his dead wife, I realize; I resent her for traumatizing Sam so that even now, more than ten years later, she resurfaces in his psyche. Andrea is dying all over again, her pain transferred to Sam. He is mumbling her name. The room feels spiked with sharp needles, poking everywhere, into my skin too.

Alan speaks to me so Sam cannot hear. "You weren't there when she . . ." he hisses. "You have no idea how bad it was."

I go back out to the nurses' station and yell until I hyperventilate. I no longer recognize to which uniform I have spoken. I no longer recognize the polite, deferential person I used to be. All I know is that Sam needs help. Fast.

"Here he is now," says a nurse, and points to a man in a white coat bustling down the hall.

Lucky for us, this doctor happens to be one of Scardino's fellows. Harold Tsai. He speedily tends to Sam, once again irrigating his bladder until the clot comes loose and Sam is calmer. Harold tells us that Sam's condition is uncommon. They don't often see it in prostectomy patients. He will brief the nurses should it happen again.

"Will it happen again?" asks Sam.

Harold shrugs. "Perhaps. Hard to say." He explains that Sam's having trouble healing because the radiation done six years ago fried the bladder's inner lining. "There's been serious insult to the area," Harold says. "Keep watch for any spasms. That's a sign that things are beginning to clog up again."

Sam thanks Harold. "You're my Tsai of relief."

Harold smiles weakly. "I've heard that before."

"We should all get some rest," I say, when Harold finally leaves.

"I'm too keyed up," says Sam.

"You need to rest," I repeat. "To get better."

"I'm never going to get better," he moans. "This illness is going to be my next career."

"See you in the morning," waves Alan to Sam. "And do like your good lady says. Get some sleep, will you?"

"You have to walk," says Nurse Linda. "That's the only way you'll heal."

"But my leg . . ." Sam protests.

"You can lean on my shoulder," says Linda. "I'll take the weight."

Nurse Linda is about forty, with shoulder-length chestnut hair. She sits beside Sam on the edge of the bed. "Come here," she chides. "Swing your legs around."

"This leg won't move," says Sam.

"That's right, just lift it up," says Linda. "There you go."

First she unhooks his catheter bag from the bed frame and hooks it to a metal pole on wheels. Then she sits beside Sam on the edge of the mattress and pulls his arm around her shoulder. Very slowly, paying no heed to Sam's groans and grimaces, she raises him to a standing position. Three tentative steps, four, five, six. . . Linda leads my husband across the room. His face is screwed up with the effort. With great difficulty, he manages to put one foot in front of the other. "Good work!" she beams as she lets him down into the chair. "The first time out's the hardest. But you did great."

Sam is winded, sweating, as if from a five-mile sprint.

"I want you sitting up this morning," Linda says. "And," she says, looking meaningfully at me, leaning against the doorjamb, "when you've rested a bit, your lovely wife can take you for another walk."

Sam nods. Okay, he'll do it. "Something to drink," he says to me.

I hand him the cranberry juice from the breakfast tray. "No," he shakes his head. "Ice."

Ice I retrieve from the kitchenette down the hall. Eyeglasses from the bedside table. Tissues from the bathroom to wipe clean the eyeglasses. His gold pen, which he suddenly must locate, I find under a pile of newspapers. The crossword puzzle in today's *New York Times*. Not that I mind fetching things for Sam. I am glad to be needed. Performing these small tasks for him makes me feel less helpless before his bodily pain and less superfluous to his grand crisis. But it's a fine line I tread, one that runs between being needed and being taken for granted. I want to be thanked. I want him to bark his commands with some appreciation of our matrimonial bond.

"I'm ready," Sam finally says. "Let's try getting as far as the hallway."

I put his arm around my shoulder, and trying to be as firm yet considerate as Nurse Linda, I attempt to pull Sam to a standing position.

"Ouch!" he shouts. "Watch out! I'm caught!"

The tip of his Johnny has somehow wound its way into my waistband. We are a comical pair, as I straighten us out and swivel so we both face the door. Sam shuffles, one foot in front of the other, his bad leg dragging, and I lead as competently as I can. I am the strong one now, and he is frail, and this bothers me more than I wish it would. It bothers me that my husband has become, physically, so utterly undone. He's a far cry, just now, from the vital, athletic man with whom I first fell in love. And then it bothers me that his frailty bothers me. Am I that unable to see beyond the myth of the strong, protective male, the one who will put his arms around *me* the better to ward off jungle beasts?

We pass the room next to Sam's, where the husband lies propped comfortably in bed, watching the television that hangs from the ceiling, and the wife is seated beside the bed, her feet in blue mules, knitting. Whenever I pass this particular room, husband and wife present this exact domestic tableau. When did they become so at ease with each other? How have they learned to take crisis in such even strides? Or are they so rigidly fixed in these postures that nothing, not even serious illness, can shake them?

Sam and I watch his feet. They make one step, two steps. I keep pace. I think about the fact that I have held up pretty well in this crisis. Certainly I have not collapsed, as was my original fear. I am stronger than I thought I was. I can get through this. I *will* get through this. One step at a time.

Approaching us is another man with the same IV getup as Sam. His arm is linked through the woman's at his side. They walk as if they are out for a Sunday stroll in the park. When they reach Sam and me, they halt.

"Prostectomy?" asks Sam.

The man shakes his head up and down. He is tanned, fit, with thin tufts of hair. "We come from Argentina," he says. "For the best surgeon."

"Argentina, that's far," I say, as if we are two couples making small talk at a party.

"For Dr. Russo," the man boasts.

His wife nods in agreement. Her face is elegantly lined. She wears a black cashmere cardigan with mother-of-pearl buttons and a matching skirt. She looks as if she'd rather be promenading the halls of Sloan-Kettering than anywhere else at this moment, and right away I decide that these two must be a model prostectomy couple. He is an oceanographer whose company is laying transatlantic fiber cable. His recovery has been much easier than Sam's has—three days after surgery and he feels no pain, his urine is nearly clear, his strength returning.

Unlike Sam, the Argentinean's operation was simple and straightforward. This is his first bout with prostate cancer, and his PSA was relatively low at 4.7.

"Good-bye," they wave merrily to us as they set off again for their walk. "Good luck."

"That's about all I can take for today," groans Sam when they round the bend and are out of sight. "Help me back to my chair."

Sam has been in the hospital for eight days—a lifetime. He can now walk unassisted around the entire floor. His scrotum has shrunk back to a normal size. His urine is clear as Chardonnay. Under his civilian clothes he's wearing his brand-new size-38 Calvin Kleins, a size larger than he usually wears, but more comfortable on his healing stitches. Alan has brought a duffel bag to the hospital room. In here we pack supplies the hospital sends home: pills for bladder spasms, constipation, anemia, and pain; gauze wrapping and paper tape to keep the catheter tube in place; hydrogen peroxide; two plastic leg bags, which Sam can strap on to his calf to catch the urine while he's out and about, and one large bag for overnight use; an extra pair of no-skid socks; a package of adult diapers.

"All set?" I say. "Ready for takeoff?"

"Call the taxi," Sam orders. "Get me a wheelchair."

Alan's leg is twitching. "I'll call the cab," he says.

And then we are piled into the back of a cab, Sam pulling up his pant leg to check on his leg bag only every five minutes, none of us talking about anything but the traffic and whether we'll make the shuttle in time.

"Here we are again," says Sam when we arrive at the airport. "Minus a prostate gland."

It's sweet, this trip home. We did what we came to do and pathology reported no cancer in the margins. We sit three abreast in the front of the airplane, like weary soldiers having won a battle, resting for the next skirmish.

Sam may be fragile and sallow-complected but he is strong in demands, not just with me but with everyone. When the flight attendant stands to demonstrate how to pull down the oxygen masks and use flotation devices, Sam interrupts. "Wait a minute," he says. "I have to use the bathroom."

She points to the SEATBELTS FASTENED sign, shakes her head. Not allowed.

Sam pulls up his pant leg to show her the plastic bag full of urine. It's true that he will never survive the flight without the bag overflowing. "Gotta go," he says in his most petulant voice. "Now."

And then he dashes by her to the bathroom up front. I take a deep breath. On this flight I can close my eyes, rest a little. But once we are home? I shudder. I cannot yet imagine. ✦

8

THE HOME FRONT

I am happy to be home. I sit on my rust-colored couch, a glass of Merlot in hand, reacquainting myself with domestic minutiae. The Mexican lovebirds I bought at a yard sale eight years ago, when I lived in Jamaica Plain. The gray-striped stone I found on the beach in Wellfleet the first year we moved in together, when we were so afraid of what the future might hold. Bright spines of books that were once his and mine and that are now ours. The wooden rocking chair we bought when we came home from Paris. We spied it out on the sidewalk in front of a used furniture store on Massachusetts Avenue and agreed right away, with equal enthusiasm, that its crisp lines and wide arms were so much more *us* than the padded gliders displayed in baby furniture stores. Without delay, we bought and upended the chair into the car, its feet facing upward, driving carefully home.

Piece by piece, bit by bit, we made a home together. When I think of the succession of rented rooms I inhabited through my twenties, restless and rootless, each time packing up in boxes my one plate and three bowls, my typewriter, my thin volumes and tattered manuscripts, I tell myself that settling down like this is no small accomplishment. Every time Sam hung a painting or I stained bookshelves we settled in a little deeper. Every Saturday morning we went out shopping together and returned with bath towels, an old library table, a toaster oven—happily surprised to find we liked the same things—we strengthened our bond. This sturdy, comfortable nest we have made together is as much our marriage as is the less tangible currents that flow between us.

I am happy to be home, but home is changed. Alan and I fit a queen-sized plastic cover over the mattress on Sam's and my bed—for accidents. Sam hires a handyman to install metal bars in the shower stall—lest he slip. And there are new smells: piss and plastic and hydrogen peroxide to ward off infections.

I place Sam's Tylenol Codeine tablet directly on the bedside table and he says, "Is that sanitary? The nurses used paper pill cups."

I place my hands on my hips. "Well, I am not a nurse. They wouldn't have let you come home unless they thought you could survive in the germ-filled home climate."

"Don't you think you should take my temperature?" he asks. "I'm feeling a little feverish."

I place my hand on his forehead. It is rather warm. But fever? He's taking the Tylenol Codeine for wound pain, for the stapled laceration still running raw down his belly. "You're dressed pretty warmly," I say. I motion to his wool sweater, wool socks, sweatpants. "Plus, the furnace is cranked."

"Where's our thermometer? Don't we have a thermometer?" I sense the beginnings of hysteria in his voice.

He won't say as much, but Sam misses the hospital: the steady routine of nursing shifts, the constant checking up on his vital signs, the never-ending supply of gauze and tiny paper cups for his pills. All those young women lifting him up in bed to put a dry towel under his bottom. The important doctor stopping in on his rounds, listening seriously to Sam's concerns.

It is new, seeing the side of my husband that needs caring from people paid to do so. Hospital personnel attending to me have always seemed brisk and distant. Even the warmest professional caretakers feel colder than people who love me: my mother arranging a room with fresh-cut flowers. No matter my complaints about my parents, past or present, I know that their interest for my well-being does not wane when a particular shift ends. No nurse, no matter her dedication, can compare. Seeing Sam's spirit thrive under medical care gives me serious pause. I realize anew how meager and insufficient was the love doled out to him at birth, and how precious the unconditional love I received—a love I no longer take for granted, and a love I am more determined than ever to pass on to my son.

Once he gets used to being at home again, Sam is largely occupied with catheter care. At night, a large plastic satchel dangles beside the bed, collecting urine. Once or twice he wakes long enough to empty his full bag into a plastic gallon jug beside the bed. In the morning, because the full jug is too heavy for healing Sam to lift, my job is to carry the gallon of yellow liquid and empty it into the toilet. Then Sam changes from his night bag to the smaller leg bag, which he wears during the day, each time washing and sterilizing with meticulous care to ward off infections. Our bathroom, which once held aromatic soaps, No More Tears Shampoo, moisturizers, and essential oils, is now littered with plastic catheter satchels drying on towel racks. Obsessed with his bodily functions, all Sam wants to talk about is fluid intake and outtake. The bathroom door is shut tight for hours at a time. At odd moments I dart in and out to use the toilet, to shower, to brush my teeth, each time feeling like an intruder. As a result, I often appear ill groomed.

This first week home, the phone rings often. People want to know how Sam is, asking when they can visit and what they can bring.

"Come over and take a walk with him," I say. "He's supposed to walk every day to help the healing." I lower my voice. "And it cheers him up to see people."

When Sam's friends come to visit, they speak in careful, whispery voices, as if expecting a fragile Sam. His old friends—the Community—pays their respects. Although we see less of Miranda and Willy and Mitchell and the others since we've married and had a child, the long-standing telephone network, which once organized demonstrations in Boston Common to protest Israel's treatment of Palestinians, now keeps abreast of Sam's health.

Miranda stands in our front hall and unwinds a bright-colored scarf from her neck.

"How *is* he?" she asks.

"Coming along," I say.

"How far can he walk?"

"Half an hour, at least. The longer the better."

"How are *you*? This is a lot for you. Have you thought about a home health aide?"

"It's not really like that," I say. "We're not really in the home health aide category." For Sam needs no help showering or dressing or getting out of bed. It's hard to explain to Miranda that what's taxing for me is that I no longer have a helpmate for home and child, and that the constant little tasks—fetching glasses of water, locating tissue boxes—wears me down.

Sam descends the stairs, catheter bag tucked unseen beneath his sweats. "Good to see you!" he exclaims to Miranda.

He's turned into an optimistic hearty type for his old comrade. Miranda's face falls in visible relief that Sam appears little changed. "You *look* great," she says. "For what you've been through."

It's only me, his intimate, who is granted the privilege of seeing Sam at his weakest and most disagreeable.

Sam is glad to see himself reflected so well in Miranda's regard. With the sure movements of the dapper man about town he was when I first met him, he dons his blue Barney's coat and a fleece hat. "Let's walk up by the mansions on Reservoir Street," he jokes. "So I can feel poor."

He takes his cane, because his leg is still weak. He holds on to the crook of Miranda's arm. I stand at the window, with Isaac, to watch my husband leave. Snowdrifts, asphalt—in this winter light, everything flattens to black and white. Once again I see my husband's vulnerability as he picks his way down the icy driveway, choosing each step with painstaking care.

For an hour or so I have only Isaac in my care. The demands of child rearing seem simple in comparison to caretaking for my blustery, kvetching husband. I still feel profoundly divided between my two boys. I can meet Isaac's demands for food and play and affection so much easier than I can satisfy Sam's enormous dissatisfactions and monumental cravings.

Yesterday, as he was going to sleep, Sam said, "My whole life, except for you and Isaac, has been a gigantic mistake."

I said nothing. I am glad not to be a mistake. I am sad about his whole life. But I can only be sad for so long. My whole life is not a mistake. I wanted to get married, and I did. I wanted a child, and I have one. I wanted to write, and I do. Maybe the problem is that Sam has not known what he wants from life?

Another day, listening to the news on the radio, he says bitterly, "People I worked with are now in the Knesset. And look at me."

"Is that what you want? A government position?"

"I don't know. Don't talk to me." He turns off the radio and shuffles back to the bathroom.

Friends urge me to take better care of myself. "You're doing everything," they say. "Do something for yourself."

They are right. I get in the habit of leaving the house at least once a day. I walk to a coffee shop or drive to a bookstore. It's a wonder to just be out in the world. Isn't it enough, I want to say to Sam, that the world, with all its petty stories, still goes on? Buses rumble, babies are born, streetlights sparkle at night. Isn't this enough?

I find myself just looking at people, wondering about their lives. In Starbucks I watch the young couple sipping lattes, their tousled heads touching as they study a thick book of tortes. Will they marry? Do they know the laws that apply when one person in a marriage irrevocably changes? Somewhere, it must be written: *He will change and you will change and this will be a trial.*

Soon enough, I go home, to the six rooms that feel, these days, apart from the world. Sam's brother Alan stays ten more days. Our meals are more festive because he is here; we drink wine and gobble sumptuous pastries. Sam and he sit side by side at Sam's computer, checking out Web sites and reading the

Jerusalem Post. They sit in the living room and converse for hours, Isaac climbing into one and then the other's lap. They talk about hardware, software, Netanyahu, Rabin, people they knew twenty years ago. The brothers' new closeness is a silver lining to our cloud. And these days, the weather is cloudy indeed.

One day I go out clothes shopping, to T.J. Maxx. I haven't bought anything except nursing bras and a few T-shirts since Isaac was born. Today I don't have anything specific in mind, and that turns out to be a problem. In the vast, overheated room, I am overwhelmed by racks. I am paralyzed between the scads of winter clearance items and the tantalizing new spring wear. I literally do not know which way to turn. Do I need a boiled wool jacket? A cotton/rayon sweater with stripes? Everything looks like a costume; nothing looks suitable.

By the time I make my way to Evening Wear, I dimly sense I shouldn't have come here alone. What's needed is for me to try on many, many styles and sizes until I find what fits and what I like, but it occurs to me that like Sam, I, too, am no longer comfortable in my own skin. I no longer have the heart to strip in the fluorescent-lit dressing room and confront the folds of my flesh in a full-length mirror.

My epiphany peaks when I reach Housewares, the tinny picture frames displayed in a crooked line. I've become a wife and a mother who puts others' needs first *all the time*. I feel like the worst female cliché. I've totally neglected myself.

A voice inside me, a voice that could belong to any woman's face in any 3 × 5 frame, says, *But you sort of have to, for now, don't you? Until Sam recovers?*

It's just so familiar, so easy, this putting another person's needs before my own, I reply to this voice. My entire upbringing as a girl and a woman trained me to do so. The baby dolls I rocked in their cradles; the cues I received from my mother, who always put us, her family, first. What was a self? For a long time I thought that having a self meant being selfish. Having struggled to find a self, to cultivate it as if it were a fragile plant in need of proper soil and climate, I am stunned to have lost it.

It's temporary. You'll get it back.

I no longer know who I am.

Caretaking without taking care, I have lost myself to my marriage. I feel under water, amorphous, literally without a definitive shape to clothe.

Four weeks post-surgery, Sam's catheter is removed. For this, a urologist is required. I drive with Sam to Mass General, to Dr. Calagari's office.

Dr. Calagari's waiting room is narrow and underheated. Ragged magazines months out of date are piled up. Nearly every chair is taken, the men pockmarked and sad, looking permanently disappointed. After a long while, Sam's name is called.

Dr. Calagari greets us at his office door. He extends a bony hand. He's dressed in the same steel gray suit he wore on our last visit. Calagari is the surgeon whom Sam elected *not* to do the prostate surgery, ostensibly because Scardino in New York had performed many more of the complicated salvage operations, but also because, well, Sam just did not feel right going with Calagari. There was the problem of his clammy handshake. And the matter of his unreal optimism. ("Erectile dysfunction," he said. "No problem. Pfizer's bringing out a new drug this spring. Just pop a pill and nothing to worry about.")

And now we expect Calagari to finish Scardino's work simply

because Calagari, the only Boston urologist who's experienced with the complicated salvage radical prostectomy, is geographically convenient.

Calagari holds Sam out at arm's length. "Well, well, my man, went all the way down to New York, did you? Time for the catheter to come out, is it? Well, well, dear fellow, we'll see what we can do. Step right in here, will you? We'll talk after."

Sam follows the stooped-back doctor into another room and I take a seat in one of the black leather chairs. On the walls, every medical diploma known to modern urology. On his desk, a framed black-and-white photo of a woman's face. She looks like Martha Graham: full sensual lips, kohl eyes, dark hair. Mrs. Calagari, circa 1970, I presume. I am trying to come up with a catty conclusion about a doctor with a beautiful wife who renders other men impotent when my husband returns.

"Well?" I say. "Did that hurt?"

"Not at all."

Calagari takes his seat on the other side of the massive desk. He twists his hands, as if shaking off the very last drop of hand washing water.

Sam briefs Calagari. "Nine carcinoma nodules," he says. "Margins were clear. Leg nerve severed; plastic surgeon required. I lost a lot of blood. Two urethral blockages in hospital; since I've been home, occasional spasms, for which I've been taking Ditrol." On and on Sam narrates, as if his very telling allows him to master the ordeal.

Calagari listens, twisting his wrists now, lips puckered. His eyes dart back and forth from Sam to me, from me to Sam.

"Well, well, I rather get the picture, my good fellow," he finally says. "I'm afraid I would have gone about things a bit differently. For example, I usually make a lateral rather than a vertical cut in the abdomen. And I never spare the nerves."

"Never?" I am astonished. Scardino made such a point of sparing half of Sam's nerve bundles, implying that sexual functioning might return.

Calagari shakes his head vehemently. "If you're going in to get the cancer out, get the cancer out, is my philosophy. And that means not leaving anything behind." He taps his hands on the desk.

"Does that mean there might be some cancer left?" I ask. "Is there a chance Scardino didn't get it all?"

"Not for me to say," says Calagari. "Besides, it's nearly impossible to predict. But yes, there is always the chance that microscopic carcinoma is still in the body. Then it's a question of whether or not it will ever become *more* than microscopic."

This is worrisome. Why didn't Scardino mention this? Scardino was so confident that he'd cut it all and given Sam a chance at potency to boot. But now I'm wondering whether Calagari might be right. If you're going to get the cancer out, get the cancer out.

"He only spared half the nerves," says Sam. "He cut the margins rather wide, he said."

"Yes, yes, I'm sure he did," says Calagari. "Now, then. Did you folks have any questions specifically for *me*?"

Sam asks about continence. Now that his urine is no longer evacuated through a catheter tube, he is once again dependent on his own body. I imagined this to be an instantaneous transition; from tube to toilet, but the urologist explains that it will take time to restrengthen the bladder and urethra. Kegel exercises two or three times a day is recommended. "At first," Calagari predicts, "you'll need eight pads a day. Then, if you do the Kegels faithfully and the urethral muscles regain strength, you can hope to decrease the pads gradually, to one or two per day."

Sam nods, taking this in. "And . . . and . . . potency?" he asks.

Calagari taps his desk, the tips of his fingers making a hollow sound. He leans back in his swivel chair, rests his two hands under his chin in a statue's pose, and stares blankly at the ceiling. "First, you want an undetectable PSA," he mutters, his words floating upward. "Then, you want to be dry. And then—an erection."

He uses the "you" in the plural form. As in "all you prostectomy patients . . . all you men . . . all you diseased and despairing."

Sam and I are literally sitting at the edge of our chairs, as if his words are oracular. "It takes time," Calagari says. He swivels around in his chair. "You'll just have to wait and see. I'm afraid I can't make any promises there."

At home, Sam stands at the toilet, pants dropped, and waits for the trickling stream. Problem is, the stream is too thin. Drip, drip, drip drops the yellow liquid. Problem is, this goes on all day and all night. Urine pools in his pad. When he walks up the stairs, drip. When he gets up from a chair, drip, drip. When he picks up Isaac, drip, drop, drip. Drip, drip when he bends to pick up a toy, gets in the car, runs to the phone.

"Goddamn it! I can't stand it! You have no idea how humiliating this is! I'm always leaking!" he yells.

"Dadda leaky," Isaac says. "Leaky, leaky."

"What's the big deal?" I say. "I leak every month. I use pads every month. You get used to it."

"This is *not* the same!" roars Sam. "This is my life now! I can't do anything! I can't go anywhere!"

"No one can tell. No one else knows what's going on but you."

"You have no idea!" he screams. "The smell! The embarrassment!" He shakes his fists at me. "I'm a grown man in diapers!"

Later, when he's calmer, he remarks: "Isaac's going to outgrow his diapers before me. Pitiful, isn't it, for a dad to use his own son's diaper pail?"

For dinner, I broil a steak. Sam's anemic since the operation, and the doctors advised iron pills, red meat. Sam jokes that you need a prescription to eat meat in health food–conscious Cambridge. To go with the steak, I boil red potatoes and fix a green salad. Sam sits at the table, fork and knife in hand, and I set a plate of food before him.

Very deliberately, he cuts off a piece of meat, which is brown on the outside, maroon on the inside. He spears it with his fork. He puts it in his mouth. He chews, he tastes, he swallows. He puts down his fork. "Cooked too long," he pronounces. "Not flavorful enough."

Ordinarily, I am not a person who sets great store on what others think of me as a cook. Nor am I a believer in "the way to a man's heart is through his stomach." I can throw together a hearty, fast meal; I like my own cooking. However, in this instance, I am crushed. I prepared the food while the baby napped. I put flowers on the table. I meant this meal to strengthen not only Sam's blood but also the good blood between us. I can see now that my expectations ran too high; I cooked this meal with the hope that it would make me feel less alone in my own house.

I take a bite from my steak. It is buttery sweet, with a hint of fresh pepper. "Tastes fine to me," I say.

"You always did like it overdone," he says, the disdainful food critic.

I push away my plate. I get up from the table. I go outside, sit on the porch steps. I don't care that it's cold and I have no coat. I sit there and I have myself a good cry, with the February moon as my witness. It's not what he thinks of the meal. It's the whole setup: me as a housewife who waits on her husband and he as dispenser of truths. It's his temper, which ranges from sour to enraged to bitter. It's my mouth, which hurts to smile and cannot speak my own unhappiness.

When did this happen? I ask myself. When did I learn to dance to the marital refrain that goes: *Where's the scotch tape?—Have you seen my tax file?—What's for supper?* I have a Ph.D. and a sheaf of literary publications to my name. I used to teach courses in the women's studies department.

I hear again the voice that I heard in T.J. Maxx, the sweet voice from the heart-shaped picture frame: *Think*, says the voice. *Think this through.*

Because he had enough money and I did not, I allowed us to make a traditional marriage. And then I had a child. We went from being comrades and lovers to gender-specific robots. Doesn't that often happen?

Yes.

We became parents, and although that was the happiest event, we got stuck: She makes the milk, he makes the money. I'll change the baby; you take out the garbage. We became too, too tired. Friendship frayed.

Don't be too hard on yourself. This is a difficult time.

Without either one of us saying a word about it, I've become food shopper, food preparer, laundress, errand runner, and chauffeur.

That can be a problem.

How much of this can I blame on my husband's illness? In my house, I suddenly find myself the lowest of the low. Double caretaker, negligible income.

A dangerous position indeed.

And now my self-worth is utterly dependent on what he thinks of my steak.

Here and there we have hopeful nights, optimistic days, but they are mostly consumer-oriented. With his money we buy a double dresser to replace the yard sale eyesores we've held onto for years. The new dresser occupies an entire wall. His and hers, constructed from the same oak. No matter that I feel us moving farther and farther apart; our socks and shirts will remain side by side. We open and close the drawers, marveling at how easily they glide. On my side I place a rose quartz crystal, meant to warm the heart, and my carved elephant box, a lucky keepsake. On his side Sam places a clock radio and a stack of old issues of *Science*.

We lie down on the bed, side by side. Light as a feather, tentative and tender, Sam strokes the small of my back. I respond to his touch, move my hips, but too soon my heart clenches and tightens into an unlucky stone.

"Got to go change my pad," mutters Sam. And then he is lost in the bathroom, occupied with his personal hygiene, that perpetual challenge.

Another optimistic day, the cold weather clearing, we buy a dishwasher.

"This should make our life easier," says Sam. "No more washing by hand."

The morning after the night we run the first load, Sam creeps downstairs to the kitchen. I find him holding up a clean dish for close inspection and beaming like someone in a Calgon ad. "It does a good job," he says, and for the first time in a long while he is pleased.

Maybe he's the one getting in touch with his inner 1950s housewife, and in the odd projections made possible by the sanctity of marriage, I have taken on that role for him.

We try out an easier life, one lived with a sturdy appliance. After breakfast I load the breakfast dishes. After lunch I load the lunch dishes. After dinner . . .

"Will you please look at what you are doing?" he says to me. He points to plates leaning against plates, bowls tipped beside cups. "Can't you see how much space you've wasted! Goddamit," he cries. With a dramatic clattering of china and cutlery, he rearranges the dishes to his satisfaction. "There," he shouts. "That's better."

Not yet satisfied, he pulls open a kitchen drawer and, still cursing, pushes aside potholders and trivets until he finds the dishwasher manual. He flips the pages until he finds the picture diagramming a dishwasher's interior. For a few long minutes he studies the page. "Look," he says, and he thrusts the manual at me. "That's the way it should be done."

I am in shock. Never in my entire life have I read a dishwasher manual and I haven't the slightest intention of doing so now. From now on I leave the dishes stacked by the sink. "Clearly, you are the expert dish loader," I say, biting off my words. "You do it then."

I confide in Rita, Isaac's beloved babysitter, who still relieves me for five hours a day. She takes Isaac to the park, speaks to him in Russian, and feeds him too many jars of pureed sweet potato.

During our family's most anxious, acute times, she feeds Sam and me, too. Tupperware containers of kasha and noodles she brings on the bus; thick slices of potato she fries in heavy oil. "Is my way," she says, putting a dish of steaming food on the table, "to take care all my children."

"Rita," I say one afternoon when Isaac's still napping. I'm home early from haunting the city and my brain smolders with sheer exasperation. "What can I do, Rita?" I say. "You see how Sam is. Unhappy, yelling, nothing I do is right. It's difficult, every day now. How long can we go on like this?"

Rita stretches her legs. "Men," she says. "Marriage," she says. "I will tell you." She has been married nearly thirty years to Benjamin, who is an engineer. They have two grown children and a three-bedroom apartment, and when he picks her up after work they stroll down my driveway holding hands.

"Every woman say the same thing," Rita tells me. "After marriage, after baby, husband never the same. He should take care of baby more, do more housework, pay more attention. Before marriage, one thing. Now is different. You have a beautiful baby—this is love. You have a nice house—this is good. You have friends—this is important. Plus, you have me, for some freedom. Go out, enjoy yourself, buy yourself a lipstick. Read your books."

She peels a clementine, offers me a slice. "But Rita," I say. "Not every husband has cancer. Look at him. The leaking, the impotency. Is it ever going to be good again?"

"You are right," she says. "This is difficult." She swallows an orange section and wipes the juice from her hands on her jeans. "The main thing is he is alive. And, you do not know what the future will be like. What about this miracle drug? This Viagra?"

"We're not sure that will work," I say.

"Americans," she says, spitting out a seed. "Everything must be fixed, everything must be perfect, everything must be good.

First, Ritalin, then Prozac, and then—Viagra. No? All these pills to get through life."

"They help a lot of people," I say.

"In Russia, we do not expect as much. Tragedy, you cannot avoid. The thing in life is to become wise. To understand everything. To give to your friends. This is what you can do." She sighs.

I remember how she left everyone and everything she knew to come to the States, how she's learned a new language, a new country, and then she helped seventy of her relatives to do the same. By comparison, what's a little lifesaving surgery from one of the best hospitals in the world?

Momentarily, at least, I am convinced by Rita. I expect too much out of marriage. I expect marriage to make my life happy and full, when in fact loving another person deeply for a long time can be guaranteed to make life more complex and multi-layered. It is this richly textured dailyness I should be encouraging, rather than the petty domestic squabbles in which Sam and I have become enmeshed. Hasn't Sam guided my slow, upward climb toward midlife from the time we met? Didn't I marry him because I believed in compromise and was ready to embrace limitation?

"Men are difficult," says Rita from across the room. "Marriage is hard. Sam and you are going through a hard time. But things will get better. You wait and see."

Things do not get better.

"I can't take it!" yells Sam. "The chaos! The mess! The disorder! My life!" We are in his office. To top it off, his printer is broken.

With that, he picks up the Hewlett Packard and throws it against the wall. Crash, bang, and the plastic cover is on the floor, the inner workings beyond repair. We turn to look at each other, both of us surprised at how things have escalated, and I see his pupils dilating with a pure blue rage.

I am sleeping downstairs, on the couch. Actually, I've been sleeping on the couch since we returned from the hospital. Those first nights Sam was too agitated for company. But now, with Sam's incontinence full blown, and his temper full fury, my sleeping apart from him feels different in intent. I am exhausted trying to meet his demands, with trying to *please* him. And yet I still want to please him. That's the sad part. I want my love to make a difference. I still believe a day will come when I will have done everything right and he will be content. For his sake, I want his painful ordeal to be over. It's terribly difficult to stand by when someone you love is suffering. But for my sake? I want to play the heroic wife, the one who nurses her husband back to well-being.

I confess to mourning the healthy body of a man who was once my lover, but even more than the physical changes, I am troubled by the change in Sam's personality. He used to be youthful and vital, full of talk and ideas, generous with praise, interested in the world. And now? His lips are pursed shut. He is consumed by his recovery.

Sad to say, I drag my body around as if it were a concrete block. The ache behind my eyes will not let me read. Every night, as I sink into cushioned sleep beneath the watchful gaze of the Mexican lovebirds, I ask myself the same questions: Am I to be forever criticized by an embittered man? Will I become a tight-jawed and frustrated woman? A reluctant matron to a damaged husband? How can I leave him? How can I stay? ✦

PART 3

EVER AFTER

9

REPAIRS

The wives are not talking. They sit at desks with foldaway arms and tidy date books. They stare at the empty stage in this chilly auditorium.

"Hi," I say to the wife on my right. She wears pins in her hair; white tennis shoes on her feet.

"First time here?" she asks.

Yes, I nod. Sam and I have decided to try a support group for prostate cancer survivors that meets in the Longwood Medical Area.

"Your husband in the men's group now?"

Again, I nod.

"Mine too." We talk some more. Her husband had his gland removed seven months ago. He was in perfect health and they only discovered the cancer when a new life insurance company refused him coverage. What a shock. She places her hand on her heart. They love their doctor.

Her name is Jeannie. They live in Cohasset.

"We went to New York," I tell her, "for a salvage. Mine had radiation six years ago. He had a recurrence. Since the operation he's been having a lot of trouble. A hard time. Me too."

She nods knowingly, comfortingly. "These meetings help my Clem a lot. See how your husband is on the ride home. See if his mood doesn't pick up."

I shake my head, skeptical. Sam has been alternately depressed and angry. Depressed—he will not leave his computer, his office; angry—he finds fault with every crevice of our house.

"Do you have kids?" I ask, just to keep the conversation going. "Grandchildren?"

"A daughter and a son. Five grandkids, God bless them every one."

"We have a toddler," I say. "A boy."

Jeannie's hand flies up to her mouth. "You're young to be going through this."

"He's older, my husband. Young to be going through this stuff but older than me." When I say this I feel young—not young and inexperienced with life the way I felt when I first met Sam and he told me about Andrea's death, but too young for the chronic ailments of old age. Too young to be the peer of retired grandparents.

Then the husbands file back into the room. An hour ago the men, all thirty of them, drooped and frowned, their hands shaking as they balanced plastic snack plates from the refreshments table. Now there is decidedly more bounce to their step. They look like a ragtag militia army, wounded but undefeated. A smirk here, an elbow jostle there, as if one has just told the other a punch line to a dirty joke.

I see Sam talking to a burly man. Sam smiling! Sam exchanging hearty handshakes. The man pats him on the back. Sam coming back to life?

"How did it go?" I say when he sits beside me, his spirits visibly lifted.

"Good. Tell you later," he whispers.

Tonight's speaker takes the podium. He darkens the hall. He narrates slides of misshapen cells. He answers questions with full knowledge of his subject and ample empathy for his patients. Sam takes notes, a student of his own calamity. *See if his mood doesn't pick up on the way home*, said Jeannie. I try not to think about the fact that we've hired a babysitter for this, a rare evening out, just to be together in a room of aging, impotent men, but there it is: my own disappointment.

In the car on the way home, Sam says, "Things have sure changed since my first go-around. Support groups? Eight years ago, when I had radiation, there were no such things as support groups. There was nothing! No one!"

"There were almost a hundred people there tonight," I reply, for the gathering of aging, impotent men is also a victory, a sign of strength.

We have crossed the river and are humming the dark and crooked streets of Cambridgeport. We pass Miranda's building, where we first met, and the marigold streetlamp under which I first gave Sam my phone number. My breath quickens a bit remembering that night, Sam's handsomeness, and my half-excited, half-anxious feeling: *Will he call?* I want to go back to the young woman I was. I want to tell her that of course he will call. He will call and call and call until she finally hears him.

Sam must be sensing my thoughts, for he says, rather wistfully: "That was a long time ago, Miranda's party. When you were young and sweet."

"And now what am I?"

"A seasoned woman."

"*Well*-seasoned," I tease. We are teasing again. He called me

161

young and sweet. My oh my, I think, it's been a long time since I've heard that tune in the air.

"Did I ever tell you what happened the first time I went for radiation treatment?"

"No. What?"

"I was taking my last few steps over to the treatment bed, when my knees buckled. I practically fell. Two technicians held me up. I had such a sense of the die being cast. This was it! I'd decided on radiation and there was no turning back."

And then we fall silent. We both think that if Sam had chosen surgery eight years ago, the cancer might not have come back.

"I'm still glad I chose radiation," Sam says with conviction. "It was the best decision I could have made at the time from what data were then available—"

"All that research you did with Terrance," I add.

"I don't regret my decision," he says rather vehemently. "I saw how the surgeons dominated the field. I read the data on survival, which was practically nonexistent, and I saw no advantage to doing surgery. Besides," he says, his voice softening, "I got seven more years of shtupping."

"Me too," I say. "Seven more years of you."

We are fast coming up on Massachusetts Avenue, the bright lights of the Middle East Restaurant glaring into my eyes. "Grab a bite to eat before we go home?" says Sam.

"Isn't there a new place in Central Square?"

In the restaurant, we sit adjacent, knees grazing. We order wine, a calamari appetizer. "I'm dying to know," I say. "About the men's group."

He picks up the long-stemmed wineglass, twirls it between thumb and forefinger. Sniffs his Pinot. "Mostly it was technical information about achieving what they call 'an erection firm enough for penetration.'"

"Really? You guys talked about sex the whole time?"

He shrugs. "Locker room talk."

"And?"

"Everyone's limp after the surgery. I suppose there are guys out there with no problem getting it up, but obviously they're not going to show up for an impotency group."

"Yeah, right."

"A lot of the guys swear by injections. There's a doctor at Boston Medical Center they all go to, a Dr. Goldstein. I guess I should try him, eventually. But there are other things to try, too. I've got to make an appointment up at MIT."

It's my turn to taste the wine, to delay my response. This is still new, being out with Sam. In the car, under cover of darkness, we softened to each other again, but really, I'm no longer used to sitting across from him and conversing. I need time to collect my thoughts. Sex? Until ten minutes ago, Sam and I haven't even *liked* each other enough. And he's become so private about his body, a site of pain and failure.

Sam clears his throat. He's waiting, I realize, for me to comment. He's said something about seeing a sex doctor. "Yeah," I say. "That would be a good idea." Do I sound too eager? Not eager enough?

"I mean, I might as well," he says. "It's been long enough."

He settles back in his chair, gets comfortable. I know that posture of his too well; one of resignation and postponement.

A few weeks later. "Watch out!" I say. Our ancient Saab almost collides with Death Wish Piano Movers.

"Just relax," says Sam. "I know what I'm doing. I wouldn't have gotten so close if the brakes weren't going again on this damn car."

"At least it's safe in an accident." I am defensive about the Saab, the used car I brought into our marriage, the car I'd bought cheap, on a whim, that was, naturally, often in the shop. The car that made Sam accuse, "You've been had! How can I trust your decision making?"

The car that made me say, "Why don't you get your own car?"

"Because I'm paying for yours!"

"If you remembered where you put your keys," I say now, "we wouldn't always be late and you wouldn't have to drive so recklessly."

"Give me a break," he says. "I agreed to try this with you."

This is our first meeting with a couples' therapist. Sam parks outside a suburban stucco house. We walk a narrow path to the side door. A thin man in his sixties emerges from a shadowy hall. His pants are belted above his waist. His shirt collar is beginning to fray.

The therapist leads us to his office, which smells musty and damp. On the walls are framed posters of classical statues, most naked and missing body parts.

Sam and I sit side by side facing the therapist, who crosses one leg over the other and assumes an alert, listening position. Sid Caesar. That's who he looks like. I expect a joke, but then I remember that our business here today is serious.

My husband, the talker, launches into a long autobiographical narrative. His first wife's illness and death. His first diagnosis and radiation treatment, his banked sperm, our infertility treatments, Isaac's birth, and then, most recently, his cancer recurrence and surgery. I see Doc Caesar's eyes open wider and wider. Sam is clearly an unusual case. The therapist shifts his weight in his chair and then shifts it back again. I look at my watch; twenty minutes have passed. Listening to my husband tell the whole fantastic arc of his medical life, I remember what attracted me to him. The sheer drama he lived. The grief I wanted to assuage.

And now it is my drama, too. And who will comfort me?

During a pause, when Sam's headlong speech seems to be winding down, I manage to say, "It's been difficult for me, too." Isn't this part of my frustration with Sam? That his suffering takes up so much room? He's the one with the disease; I am merely supportive.

I tell Doc Caesar about how my husband yells at me for how I load the dishwasher, for how I cook his steak. I tell him how I am found guilty for the dust balls under the bed, guilty for the stacks of mail, guilty for the messes of toys. I hear the nagging whine my voice has taken on. I have become a complaining wife. I stop my tirade, take a deep breath. "It's his rage," I say. "I know he's angry at what happened to him but he's got to stop taking it out on me."

Doc Caesar's bushy eyebrows go up. "What about what she says?" he says to Sam, referee-like. "What about you taking your anger out on Karen?"

"I know it's been hard on her," says Sam. "I know. And I haven't always been, well, sensitive to that. She's been very supportive, very brave." My husband turns to look at me in the chair beside him and it's as if a glass wall between us has come down. I see a dull sadness in his eyes that makes me feel pity. I suddenly see how the pain he's caused me by the pain he is in has created a weird kind of closeness.

"Who else is he going to take it out on?" Doc Caesar asks me. "You're the one who's closest to him."

It takes two more sessions until I can look Sam in the eye and say, "Your demands about keeping the house neat and orderly— I hate it. I feel controlled by it. It's an impossible task with a toddler about."

Still the referee, Doc Caesar turns to Sam. "Well?"

"With everything so disorganized with my body, I crave domestic order," says Sam. "It's the one thing you can do to help me, Karen."

I sigh. If this is what the man wants, I suppose I should be less stubborn in giving it to him. "All right," I say. "I'll try to keep things neater. But—you're going to have to try, too."

I grit my teeth and spend entire mornings cleaning closets and cupboards, throwing out bent spatulas, mold-covered mittens, a broken dump truck . . . even an ankle-length skirt belonging, I believe, to Andrea. I fill five plastic garbage bags with things we don't need, including issues one to twelve of *Political Science Today* from 1979.

I drive to a high-end hardware store where I purchase plastic bins in several sizes, a shower organizer, a mail sorter, and a shelving unit on wheels. I am in a fury. I buy a beveled glass cabinet for the bathroom wall, a metal wineglass rack to hang beneath the kitchen cabinet. Why did I never do this before? How did I ever function in so much disorder?

My house is a scrambled jigsaw puzzle. Drawer by drawer, I will fit the pieces back together.

When I show Sam the place we'll store onions, he is so grateful. When I open a cabinet and show him the maps I've folded and held together with a rubber band, he becomes happy and calm.

"I can think now," says my husband. "I feel better when I know you're keeping things under control."

"If you're happy, I'm happy," I say.
He takes my hand. Warmth travels up my spine.

Tonight is a special night at the support group. No lecture. Instead, men and women meet in separate groups to discuss our concerns. I am looking forward to this meeting. Finally, I think, I can connect more deeply with the wives, with other women who share my concerns.

Right away I spot Jeannie, sitting near the door. I plop right down next to her. "How are you doing?" I say.

"Fine, just fine," she beams.

A social worker who wears a lot of makeup is in charge tonight. We sit in a circle and introduce ourselves. I who have not taken my husband's surname am struck by how unselfconsciously each woman introduces herself by husband's date of diagnosis, husband's date of treatment, and husband's present PSA status. Almost as an afterthought do we learn her name: Holly, Irma, Nance, Abigail, Bea.

"My Norm had radiation six years ago, knock on wood," says a tiny woman with a large hunchback. "My Norm's past 80. We don't have no problems. I do whatever he needs, take care of him like I always have. We take each day for what we can."

Take care of him like I always have. Is my problem with Sam that I don't *expect* to take care of him? That our relationship is based on such newfangled notions as respecting each other's autonomy?

"You've got to love them a lot," says a woman wearing a cameo brooch on her navy blue sweater. "They've just been through this horrible scare, and this painful operation, and they're feeling bad about, you know, their manhood, and what I keep telling myself is you got to love them a lot. When Blaine got out of the hospital, I cooked all his favorite dishes, tried to make him feel special. Every time he said to me, 'I'm not a *man* anymore,' I told him, 'That's not important. You being here with me is important.'"

Eyes shift across the circle; glances are exchanged.

"We been married forty years," says one woman. She has three gold teeth and a heavy accent I suppose to be Greek. "When we were young—we had plenty. We got five children, twelve grandchildren. Now, it's okay. We just happy he alive."

Around the circle, heads nod in agreement. "Cuddling," says a woman wearing a sweater embroidered with bold roses. "We cuddle now, and we're close, emotionally. That's what's most important."

"Besides," says a woman wearing black pumps, "there's plenty of other ways to—improvise."

More agreement; then a shriek of laughter from Norm's wife.

"They *think* we mind more than we do," says Blaine's wife. "Really, it's about their manhood. Frankly, I have to say I know a lot of women who envy my situation. *They* only do it to please their husbands."

The room is quiet. I am listening, fascinated to hear about others' marriages, especially those from a generation older than mine. These wives all seem solid. Solid and steadfast. Listening to them makes me feel almost ashamed. I resent cooking for my husband and I want more than a cuddle. I cuddle with my child. From my man I want something, well, something more forceful.

"I'm happy my husband is alive," I say to this group, choosing my words carefully. "And cuddling is important. But it's a loss, his impotency. A loss for us both."

Then Jeannie speaks up. Jeannie of triple chins and a Snoopy sweatshirt. "Clem went to a specialist at Boston Medical," she says. "Got him on injections, which work like a charm." Her cheeks flush pink.

I've heard about penile injections and they sound gruesome. I fire questions at Jeannie.

"Do the shots hurt?"

"Not much."

"How long before they start to work?"

"Twenty minutes or so."

"Is it pleasurable for him?"

She smiles, all dimples. "Afterward, he's a happy camper."

"How long does it last?"

When Jeannie starts to crack up, giggling like a teenager, I see I have been all wrong about her, relegating her to a tidy domestic old age; all wrong about desire and appearance, wrong about desire and aging, for this sixty-something woman is having a grand old time in bed.

"Only problem is," she says, her stomach jiggling with laughter. "He stays up for two hours at least. We go to bed early, turn off the phones, and afterward we hide under the covers, waiting for it to go down."

Again, we see Doc Caesar. "Well, you two seem to be making a lot of progress," he says.

Sam beams.

"Doing any writing?" Doc Caesar asks me.

I shake my head no. Instead of writing I have been trying to be a better wife. The terms of our City Hall wedding seem to have changed. Whereas then I believed that an unconventional ceremony would lead to an unconventional relationship, one where I could remain free from matrimonial bondage, that no longer feels true. Sam became ill. We did not account enough for this calamitous change. Never did I imagine that a sick Sam would so fiercely crave domestic order. Did he know? Could he have warned me?

Trying to be a better wife, I cooked white trout and rice, roast chicken with garlic, polenta with porcini mushrooms. I researched stain removal. I wore lipstick around the house. "You're looking good!" I told Sam at every opportunity. "I love you."

I saw his hackles go down. I stopped hearing yells and reprimands. I got called "sweetheart" again and got a lot of hugs.

Now, Sam puts his hand over mine.

"My book's about to come out," I say. "I should be doing publicity. Setting up readings, that kind of thing. But it's hard to find the energy."

Doc Caesar's eyebrows go up. He looks at Sam. "Tell me you're proud of her."

"I'm proud of her," says Sam. His hand presses hard against mine and I'm glad he's proud, and I'm proud to be, at long last, a published author, but anything resembling a professional life feels so distant from the domestic tangle in which I've been mired.

"Can we talk about the rage?" I say. "It's been better, lately, but I feel it's only because I'm doing everything he wants. It's a little bit like walking on eggshells."

Our therapist looks down at his untied laces.

"I'm doing better," protests Sam. "I haven't had an outburst in—I can't remember when."

"Can we agree, please," I plead, "in this room, the three of us, that it is not okay to yell at me?"

"Men do get angry," ventures Doc Caesar. "Women, too. But men, especially men in your husband's situation. You've got to take his anger less personally. Be more like a duck. Let his words slide off your back."

At home, I do not feel like a duck. I am angry with Doc Caesar for not taking my side against Sam's anger. *We should have gone to a woman.* I was too careful to make sure *Sam* would feel comfortable with the therapist. And now we're stuck with a traditionalist.

I think about some other things, too. Much as I try, I hate housekeeping. I hate the tedium and the endless repetition. Isaac can undo in five minutes what I do in an hour. I think of my mother, who was what you might call a relaxed housekeeper. Among the household skills she passed down to me were: Buy drip-dry instead of ironing; never buy white upholstery or carpeting, for it shows the dirt. My mother, who worked full-time in literacy programs, raised three kids and was active in womens' "consciousness-raising groups" in the 1960s. I think of Sam's mother at the University of Chicago, where she and Saul Bellow were the prize students of Thornton Wilder. She wanted to be an anthropologist and live on a reservation. Instead she became a doctor's wife. She was consumed with fund-raising for Israel. She died with a spotless white carpet and all her linens folded neatly on the shelf.

I am loyal to my mother's practice. I will not sacrifice myself to my house. More important, I am loyal to the witch I was as a girl. I make a pact with myself: If I am going to be a traditional, take-pride-in-my-home type of wife, I can do it only for short stints. Sort of on a consultant basis.

I tell Sam I think we should cut back on our sessions with

Doc Caesar. All right, he says, sounding relieved. Could it be that he, too, has misgivings about the change I've forced myself to undergo?

I call a cleaning service. The service will clean our house three times for the same money we pay Doc Caesar for one session. After their first visit, Sam and I walk from room to room looking in amazement at dust-free surfaces and spot-free appliances.

I call up local bookstores, clinics, and colleges. "I have a book coming out," I say. *"The Pregnancy Project: Encounters with Reproductive Therapy.* From Duquesne University Press. That's D-U-Q-U-E-S-N-E. And, also, I'd like to do a reading, please."

Some places actually say yes. I call my editor and we talk.

I cook a large pan of lasagna that will last us the week.

In one of our last conversations with Doc Caesar, Sam exhibits a profound linguistic change. He speaks a simple, declarative sentence: "I want a Porsche."

"A Porsche!" I am outraged. "How much do those things cost?"

"I think that's the first time I've actually begun a sentence with 'I want,'" Sam says, ignoring me, pleased with himself.

"That your heart's desire?" asks Doc Caesar.

"I want a Porsche," says Sam again. I see him taste the words in his mouth. "I think I've wanted to say that for a very long time."

"Why do we need such an expensive car just to transport us from place to place?" I persist. "We already have the Mazda; the family car."

Sam inherited some money from his mother and invested it well. The funds have grown. We regard them as a safety net, and a Porsche would take a significant bite out of them. But it's not whether we can afford a Porsche or whether Sam is being impetuous, it's that whatever our financial reality, I would have trouble justifying a luxury car.

The room goes silent. I suddenly notice that the poster on the opposite wall—a headless statue with anatomically correct male genitalia—is crookedly hung. Dust motes float up from the yellowing paperbacks on the floor. Doc Caesar and Sam turn to me with the same look of wonder and disbelief in their eyes.

The following Tuesday a gigantic flatbed truck backs into our drive. It's the folks from Special Olympics, to whom Sam has decided to donate our other car, a twelve-year-old Saab Turbo. The idea of a fast, sleek Porsche hangs suspended in the air above our driveway. But it is only an idea; a wish, like wanting to climb Machu Picchu. In the meantime, he's browsing car magazines. "How about a BMW?" he says.

"Too yuppie," I say.

"A Volvo?"

"Too conservative."

"There's one car I'm not buying. That's a Saab."

"That's for sure."

Owning this Saab has been like standing in quicksand; every chunk of money put into repairs was another six months before we could let it go. For years, whenever I argued that we should cut our losses, put the car up for sale, Sam's response has been: "What makes you think any one else wants it?"

And now a great chain is attached to the Saab's rusted frame. I stand in the open doorway, holding Isaac to my hip. My son, whose vocabulary for heavy machinery is ever advancing, says, "Mama, truck! Flatbed truck! Hookup!"

The winch pulls up our old whale by the nose and plunks it down none too gently on its tilted metal bed. Believe me, I am happy to see that car leave. I hope for smoother driving ahead with Sam. I hope for easier chapters in our marriage. But right now I am surprised to feel sentiment for its rusted tin and cracked leather. This is the car in which I drove my single-girl belongings to the saltbox house of my married life. The car Sam and I drove weekends to Wellfleet. The car I drove the day I found out I was pregnant with Isaac.

"Good-bye Saab," I say.

"Bye-bye." Isaac waves a tiny hand.

"I hope this is the end of our sob story," quips Sam.

And then the truck lurches forward. ✦

10

WITHOUT SEX

The night is unseasonably warm. Outside our window, the lilac buds are getting ready to open. I strip to my salmon-colored T-shirt and slip into bed beside Sam. Like bears who sense, by some inner timing, hibernation's end, Sam and I have decided that tonight is our night.

Tentatively, I kiss his lips. Tentatively, he reaches for my breast.

We lie on our sides, breast to chest, pelvis to pelvis, in earnest about tonight's deed, a sort of second wedding night with me as the eager bride and he the shy groom. My hand through his hair; his hand on the small of my back, we mold our bodies one to the other, snaking our wet tongues to coax desire's spell.

The sheets remain cool.

I touch the fine tendons on his neck. I trace circles around his nipples, tangle my pinky in his chest hairs. Again I press my mouth to his. Ever so gently and then not so gently I stroke his belly.

Minutes pass. I am afraid to reach lower.

Finally, Sam guides my hand between his legs. And then I know too.

"It hasn't been long," I say quietly. "The doctors said it could take months and months to get it back."

"It's been four months," he says. He rolls onto his back.

My hand is still moving up the outside of his thigh, across his hip. "Want me to try—"

"Don't."

I pull away. Inside my mouth, a souring.

We do not talk about our botched lovemaking. What is there to say? These things happen. Too soon to tell. Not: Doesn't look good. Not: You have erectile dysfunction.

A Saturday night sometime later. Our child asleep, the dishes washed, Sam and I tiptoe, like conspirators, up the spiral staircase. I carry two shot glasses, Sam carries the bottle of Glenfiddich.

We sit cross-legged on our unmade bed and he raises his glass. "To us."

"To life, with an undetectable PSA forever after." I stretch my legs, flex my ankles, nestle my feet along the soft jean of his calf. "Tell me," I say to my husband, for no reason other than it's the first thing to pop into my head, "about the best sex you ever had."

He looks dubious.

"Besides with me, of course," I add.

"The best sex I ever had? Let me think." He leans back against the headboard and drains his glass.

"It would have to be Jerusalem in the seventies," he begins, his voice slow as memory. "When friends walked in and out of each other's apartments, and dinner went on for hours, sometimes from apartment to apartment, and you could never be sure who you would end up with that night."

"When you lived with many skylights," I say, for I know about this mythical apartment of Sam's single days, before he met Andrea, even.

"In the garden where the nightingale sang," he adds.

"Who was she?"

"Sarah, I think. We spent seventy-two hours together, mostly pinned to my mattress. She was American, traveling, and she had a bag of hashish. She said from the moment she lay eyes on me at Eli's, she knew I'd be a great lay. She was so—crazy. She had beautiful breasts. That was the night I discovered I could stay hard after coming."

He covers his eyes with his hand. "Look at me now. I'm sorry, Karen. I've become a miserable wretch."

I touch his wrist. "It's okay."

"No, it's not okay. I'm not the virile hunk you thought you were marrying."

"I didn't think you were such a virile hunk."

"You didn't?"

"I mean, I did, but that's not why I married you."

"Why'd you marry me?"

I stretch out beside him, leg to leg, arm to arm. I hold out my empty glass, which he refills. "Because I wouldn't be bored," I say.

"Mitchell and his ontological depth."

"Something like that."

"You certainly got what you bargained for."

"Maybe I wanted to rescue the sad widower stuck in a dingy apartment," I say. "You know, the maternal in me."

177

"Before you met me," he says, "you were sitting in the dark and walking into walls."

"That's not entirely true," I protest. "Just because I *seemed* dreamy. I functioned pretty well. I worked three jobs, had an active life . . ."

"And you were spacey."

"I'm communing with higher spheres."

"I rest my case."

"Why did you marry me?" I've never asked this before, I realize, so intent was I on pursuing him. "Because I was lost? Because I wanted you?"

He takes another swig of the scotch, shifts his weight so that he is resting on one elbow, showing me his elegant profile.

"You were a soothing woman and a good person, capable and smart. I wanted to help you become a writer. . . ."

"I already was a writer."

"I wanted to give you more opportunities to write. I *believed* in you. I loved you. You were young and sweet."

"And now?"

"It's still true."

And then he is tracing the bone at the bottom of my throat.

"Let's get under the covers and hold each other," he whispers. "Can we do that? Can we just do that?"

Like that, we fall asleep.

Masters of denial, Sam and I do not mention our sex problem. Because that is what sex has become: a problem. We are busy. We are tired. We would rather read, talk, watch TV. Who needs sex?

178

Not me. I will read far into the night and eat bonbons to my heart's delight. I will wear only baggy clothing. I am done with being hot and bothered for the mere exchange of bodily fluids. Who needs the body anyway, with its unceasing demands to be fed, washed, touched? I will devote myself exclusively to the ethereal and the companionable.

But a time comes—one week, two weeks—when Sam and I, by mutual consent, decide it is time to try again.

I've lit a candle. I've purchased a bottle of almond massage oil. "Lie down," I say. "Tonight I'll be your geisha girl."

He lies down across the bed, still dressed. "Everything off," I command.

I straddle his back and drip on the oil. His skin is thirsty and cool to my touch. I knead his shoulders and press his blades, trying to ease the heaviness that permeates his body. With the palm of my hands I press hard on his waist, pull the skin from his bones until he groans, faintly, expressing pain or delight. Under me he is warming. I close my eyes and rock on his back.

And then he is on top of me and we are moving together with the moans and rhythms of old, our breath quickening. Too soon it is over for me, and over for him as well. He never sprang to life, we both know, not even the tiniest rise.

I let out a deep breath. "That was something."

"I'm glad for you." He turns his head away. "I feel like an amputee with a phantom limb. I can still sense what it's supposed to do."

And then, exhausted from his conjugal efforts, he is fast asleep. But it is a troubled sleep, punctuated by coughs and turns.

I lie awake and stare at the ceiling. I, too, am troubled. I am in shock to lose the power I first discovered at age thirteen when I slow-danced with Danny Mandel at a boy-girl party in his parents' finished basement, surprised to find a stick pressing against

179

my leg. And then with a boyfriend, boyfriends, the confidence I gained when again and again I could make his desire so visible. And now I have lost my prowess, at least around Sam—the ability to dramatically alter male physics by my mere proximity.

May, June, July, the days swelter, the nights are long and lovely. Sam and I do not touch. Touching reminds us of loss and failure.

"Do you feel like he's less of a man?" Doc Caesar asks me. We are seeing our therapist again. "Well, no," I say, perhaps too quickly. Aren't I more sophisticated than to believe that masculinity means getting it up?

"I still see him as a man," I say. For it's true he looks like the man he always was: a bearded, barrel-chested baritone. "Besides, we have affection," I say, echoing the women I met in the support group. "We have companionship. I'm happy he's alive."

"I feel less than," says Sam. "Not just the erections—everything. I'm not active at the lab, but what am I doing? Where is my power? My potency in the larger sense? I feel *in*-valid. Invalid." He sinks back in his chair, his head falling toward his chest.

In public, I am loyal to Sam, but many nights now I am unfaithful. In sleep I dream of a lover who speaks with an Italian accent; a lover whose skin tastes like anise; a lover with Mick Jagger lips. Each one is healthy, strong, and most of all, desiring of me. I wake, moist. I reach for Sam and then remember where I am and whom I am with and all that has happened.

I think again about the long-married women in the support group, the ones who say sex doesn't matter. Are they telling the truth? Perhaps they never liked sex. Or is it that I came of age in the 1970s: the pill, rock 'n' roll, make love not war? To deny your desire was to forget your body, that real self. Educated, white, middle-class, I felt beholden somehow to offset the thousands of years that women—corseted, foot-bound, veiled—lacked for pleasure. We free women would come and come in a great frenzy of cries and froth until our sisters in their graves moaned with happiness.

One night when I wake, Sam's side of the bed is empty. It's two o'clock in the morning. I sense trouble. I glide through the house, my nightgown trailing, and climb the back stairs to Sam's office. He is seated on his ergonomic chair. He is staring, blankly, at his computer.

Nubile Girls! Wanton Women! On the screen, the bodies are curvaceous and swollen, absolutely lurid.

"I'm trying to believe it," he says, gesturing to his open bathrobe. "Nothing. Absolutely nothing is happening to me."

I touch his shoulder.

"Don't," he says. "I've been in denial, expecting my erections to come back on their own. But I have to accept that it's not going to happen on its own. I might as well start looking into the gadgetry to find something to satisfy you."

"Satisfy me?" I snap. I am suddenly angry at the way he makes love sound like a chore—like taking out the trash. Besides, it's the middle of the night, my least favorite time to be awake. In a few short hours our alarm-clock child will sound and I will be thrust into the day's whirl. "When have I put any pressure on you?" I say. "Don't do it for me if it's such a burden."

He swings around in his chair, bathrobe flapping. "Can't you take yes for an answer? I told you I'm impotent. I told you I was going to do something about it."

"Don't yell! Will you please stop yelling?" I yell.

"I'm not yelling!" he yells back. "What is wrong with you?"

"Can't you see the position you put me in? I don't want the guilt."

He jumps from his chair, shakes his hands at the low ceiling. "What do you want me to say? I *am* impotent. I am impotent. As in can't get it up, limp dick, severe erectile dysfunction. Do you want me to write it out eight hundred times? *I am impotent. Sam is impotent.*

"I'm sorry."

"That's what you call being supportive? Saying you're sorry?"

"What do you want me to say?"

"Do you have any idea . . ." he wails. He is scrunched up, his arms folded together like a grotesque amphibian, his words choked in near sobs. "Do you have any idea how painful this is?"

One sunny day soon after this, I do what any good wife would do. My hands shaking on the steering wheel just the tiniest bit, I drive to Brookline, where I climb the stairs to Grand Openings, a sex shop run by and primarily for women. When I open the door, a little bell rings. Over to me walks a young woman clad in a black miniskirt and a chartreuse blouse. I explain to her my predicament and my husband's predicament, sprinkling my explanation with medical terminology and looking straight into her midnight-blue mascara eyes instead of at the shelves across the room that display, I saw immediately upon entering the store, dildos of every size and color.

"Mmmnn," she says. She places her index finger on her chin, thinking. "You say that—"

"He has a penis," I say. "That's not the problem. He still has one. It just isn't working very well at the moment."

She gestures prettily to the display shelf. "You might want—"

I am across the room in one second flat, to stand before the exotic growths that sprout from silicone pedestals: a lipstick the color of bubble-gum; a massive snake colored like the Mediterranean; a rod as dark as a disco. . . . How to choose?

"It's all a matter of personal preference," says the helpful salesgirl. She lifts up a strictly Caucasian model. "This one is very popular."

She sees me noticing the tiny price tags with not-so-tiny prices. "That," she says, pointing to a mushroom-topped speckled variety that costs $19.95, "is a good first-timer. But like I said," she shrugs, "it all depends on what you like."

I like flesh. I like Sam. I like to be filled. In the end I choose one that reminds me of my husband. Except that it is black. Not black like an African-American, but black like slate. Blacker than our bedroom when all the lights are out. It is six inches long and one-and-a-quarter inches in diameter. I pay $22.95, plus tax.

"Wow," says Sam when he sees what's inside the paper bag. "Let's take it for a test drive."

Right there in our kitchen, sitting in our straight-backed chairs, we lean into one another and kiss for a long, sweet time, the full four minutes until I must leave to pick up Isaac from day care.

Later that evening, we test drive. We are a little giddy with anticipation. We kiss, sitting up to hold each other, unsure how we will fit. We are falling together onto the bed when it suddenly occurs to me that I am in bed with one man and two penises: a real one that never goes up and a fake one that never goes down.

"Where is it supposed to go?" Sam says, his voice muffled.

"On top of the real one?" I giggle nervously. "Is that redundant?"

"Come here."

He lies on top of me, awkwardly holding the long-tipped tool above his crotch. I close my eyes and fantasize that it's really Sam entering. Although the lovely rippling sensations are real enough, I can tell the difference. When I come, I'm released into sorrow, hot tears running down my cheeks in grief for Sam's lost burrowing.

Now comes a time when my husband is once again my lover. He wants only to please me. Urged on by my enthusiasm, Sam's hands become expert explorers, finding inside me a soft padded place that he presses and presses to make me gasp. He tongues with new proficiency.

No longer do I ask, "Was it good for you, too?"

"Your pleasure is my pleasure," Sam says.

At first, I revel in this change. Whereas before, orgasms were negotiated and paced, now they are all mine. Whereas before, one good explosion made it a night, now I discover peak after peak. No longer must I worry that he wants to go further or faster or more frequently. Now I follow only my own arc and trajectory.

"Are you taking notes?" asks Sam. "Are you getting this all down for your book?"

"It's not too private for you? You really want other people to know about this?"

"I suffer, you write," he mocks.

"Stop!" I duck under the covers. "Don't say that."

"Think of the possibilities," he crows. "We are living in a non-phallocentric household."

"No more legitimized rape?" I say from under the sheet. "No more linear thinking?"

"That's us, babe."

I stick out my head. "Don't get too self-congratulatory. You still think like a guy. You still love tools and cars. You can't undo a lifetime of gender privilege with one operation."

"Give me a chance. I'm just getting used to my new identity."

"I'll believe it when I see it."

"You're seeing it."

"Oh yeah?"

"Don't be so suspicious. If a tree falls in the forest and there's no one to hear it, is it still a man's fault?"

One night, in the middle of my sensual feasting, I feel Sam heat up and his breath quicken to a rhythmic pant. He is rubbing his pelvis along my stomach. I feel his torso tense, and although there is no hardening or jism, there is a definite series of short spastic releases.

"Whew," he says. "That was . . . that was . . . I guess I came."

"What was it like?"

"Weird. Unexpected. Delicate and subtle, like a fine bouquet. A sprinkling of Northern lights, so faint in the sky so as to be barely visible."

"You're making it up," I say. "You're performing."

"Merely exaggerating. It wasn't like anything I had before, but not bad."

I buy a dress to wear to our friends' summer wedding, an afternoon party to be held in a formal garden. The dress is pale yellow, flimsy, a French country cut. When I come home from shopping I try it on. In my full-length mirror I see how beautifully translucent is the fabric, a rayon blend, and how well it drapes, smoothing and thinning.

Suddenly I want to feel thirteen again, standing in my old living room to model a party dress for my father the night before I lose my innocence slow-dancing with a boy. I want to feel all grown-up, beautiful and seductive. I want to feel the ardor of Sam and me at the beginning, when it was dangerous for us to be together behind a closed door.

Instead, I walk downstairs, to my own living room, wearing nothing but the dress. I stand in a beam of sunlight so that Sam can see my legs all the way up, my full breasts.

"Oh," he says. "Don't you look . . ." he gets up from the chair where he sits, reading the newspaper. He walks toward me, as if in slow motion, and I know from his rueful smile that just now my shape as a woman pleases him entirely.

I still have my reflexes from the old days. I am still hoping. I still expect him to walk right up to me, pupil-dilating eyeball to eyeball, joking, "Let's get something straight between us."

Halfway across the room, he grimaces in pain.

When he reaches me, he raises his hand in a gesture that says, *What's the use?* "Just the littlest bit, and then I lost it," he says.

Our friends want Sam to marry them. This is permissible in Massachusetts, where anyone can obtain a one-day license to perform a marriage ceremony. Sonia and Bruce look up to Sam and me, and to our relationship, which Sonia praises as a match between disparate strengths and weaknesses. Sam introduced them, four years ago, and they have been together ever since. They are thirty-four.

Sam writes a heartfelt ceremony in which he calls marriage a place where each person can become his or her true self. He describes marriage as a worthy discipline. He wishes the newlyweds much happiness and joy.

"I thought you didn't believe in marriage," I say when he reads a draft to me. I am astonished at his sincerity. "You never gave our wedding this much care."

"My views have changed," he says. "Don't you see that I can say all this stuff *because of* what I've learned about myself with you?"

"We never had a real wedding."

"We were going to have a party in the spring," he reminds, gently. "But then my mother died."

"I know," I say. "It doesn't matter anymore." And really, it doesn't. Especially when I can tick off an entire hand's worth of extravagant weddings we attended for couples who are since divorced. I'd rather enjoy my extravaganzas day to day, month to month.

Sam goes back upstairs to write more of the ceremony. Time for me to straighten the kitchen: sweep the floor, wipe down counters, screw the top back on the mustard jar. These domestic duties no longer require much of an effort on my part, so automatic have my motions become. Tonight my mind is on couplings, past and present, real and hypothetical. Sonia and Bruce, at the beginning of their union, make me speculate.

I think of Jerome, my boyfriend from college who came to visit me in Jamaica Plain. No longer in contact with him, I have, over the years, seen his poems appear in journals. To me, he's the same plaintive, hermetic Jerome. The same suffering-for-transfiguration kind of guy. And when I close the journal, I reel into the street with the same heady rush I used to feel when I was around him.

I caught a glimpse of Jerome not too long ago, across Massachusetts Avenue. The same leather jacket, the same purposeful gait, the same bemused, bewildered expression on his face. His hair had thinned. He'd put on weight. Many cars and passersby were between us. I was steering Isaac along the sidewalk. There was no question of conversation.

Nevertheless, I received a jolt. First, that a person I once knew so intimately and felt such passion for could now be a complete stranger on the street. Second, that I could still have been with him. I could still be wondering what woman he's with when he's not with me. I could still be the woman *with* the writer and not the writer herself. I scoop crumbs off my kitchen counter and into my hand. How wrong for me to be with Jerome. That is a role for another woman entirely.

And I think of Theo, the man I went out with for about six months before meeting Sam. Theo was a decent guy, but he was adamant about not having children. Theo was restless. He made his living as a carpenter, but what he really wanted, he claimed, was to hike the Appalachian Mountain Trail from start to finish and buy a farm in rural Maine and trek Nepal. These are not goals or even dreams of mine. Theo and I parted amiably enough. A few years back I received a postcard with a picture of a mountain in Montana. Theo drew an arrow to a spot halfway up. He'd built a cabin there. I could not imagine myself living in that kind of isolation, no bookstores or restaurants or neighbors for miles, long cold winters with ice on the panes, no child. I unload my dishwasher dish by dish. How wrong for me to be with Theo. That is a role for another woman entirely.

I think of Jonathan, a chemist who worked on rocket fuel for the Department of Defense and who told me, on our third date, that all artistic pursuit is nothing but the ego's defense against neurotic conflict. Wrong, and wrong. And Tom, who worked on wind tunnels and liked to dance to reggae music. Tom was sweet and sweet on me when we were twenty but had no real opinions for which to stand up, so that I was never sure who was really there. Tom was not right either.

In my kitchen, I throw out the used coffee filter, then grind fresh beans for the morning. In the morning Sam and I will rise and pad downstairs for our brew. He will toast frozen waffles for Isaac and take down clean cups from the cupboard. He will kiss me good morning, tell me the wedding ceremony is almost done. He will describe for Isaac the matching tuxedos they will wear, and he will make it sound so appealing, like a game of dress-up, that Isaac will ask to drive with his dad to the rental store. While they are gone I will indulge in a few things: a long shower, an even longer phone conversation with my mother.

I look around the home Sam and I have made together—the books on the shelves, the paintings on the walls, the scuffed wood furniture—and I feel right about my life. With Sam, I have become a better citizen: one who votes, pays taxes, and contributes to charity. With Sam, I celebrate the Jewish holidays with meaning and feel identified as a Jew. With Sam, I can write. With Sam, I can parent a child.

The picture of my life with Sam is by no means perfect. But it is *my* picture. Within its frame I can be both mother and writer. Both wife and independent woman. Both mate and friend. For tonight, this is enough.

I meet my Sam in our bedroom. "Hi," I say. "Long time no see."

I wrap my arms around the warm, solid trunk of my husband,

who has given me so much. His chest rises and falls with a steady, consoling rhythm, one on which I can rest my head. I place my ear over his heart; there, too, I feel a steady beat.

Sonia and Bruce's wedding day is picture perfect. Their ceremony includes Isaac, who pulls down the aisle a red wagon holding two gigantic stuffed gorillas. I stand beside Sam in my yellow dress and read from the *Song of Songs*. Sam looks wise and rabbinical in his finery, and he speaks eloquently. Here he is potent: joining two people in holy matrimony and making community of the wedding guests.

The ceremony over, Isaac restless, I walk him over to a grassy knoll where he can run with the other kids. People are gathered around Sam, praising his speech, and I am glad to let him sop up the accolades. I am content here with the sun warming my face and my choice of delicacies from the appetizer table.

A man walks up to me. He has a ponytail and, behind his wire-rimmed glasses, eyes like blue beach glass. He is drinking champagne. He tells me he works with Bruce at their dot-com. "Are you enjoying yourself?" he inquires.

"My shoes hurt," I say, motioning to two-inch heels. "I'm not used to being around so many people. It's a beautiful day, though, a beautiful wedding."

"Bruce is a lucky guy," he says wistfully. "Weddings make me feel like I'll never find anyone."

It's been a long time since I talked to someone new. A long time since I got that expectant feeling in my gut of a new world about to unfold. Yet I'm hesitant before this man. My flirting skills are rusty. Who am I to start something I cannot finish? And do I even want to fall into that new, dizzy world? What makes me think that the picture of my life would be better with this particular person? Afraid is what I am, even if I feel too often these days that my husband no longer wants me. Or he wants me and cannot have me. Or he can have me without wanting me. It is all quite confusing, especially when I am too aware of my waist thickening.

And then Sam appears at my side, places his arm around my waist with a territorial flourish. He hands me a cracker. "Have you tasted the pâté? Divine."

Three glasses of champagne later, Sam and I are sitting at the head table, under the tent. Sonia is resplendent in her bridal gown. Bruce is expansive, shaking everyone's hand, leaning toward Sonia, his face ecstatic. Sam and I sit, our legs touching, a bit electrified in the newlyweds' reflected glow.

Sam leans closer, his breath in my ear, whispers: "You look scrumptious, my dear. I wish I could do something about it!"

I lean into his side. I will never leave him. ✦

11

HYDRAULICS

My mouth is on his when the Viagra kicks in. He pushes me away. He clenches his shoulders and jerks forward his head. A loud sneeze erupts. He raises his hand to his nose, trying to stop the flow, but it is too late. His body is heaving and convulsing uncontrollably, and he is crying, "Oh! Oh! Oh!" and then a long stream of yellow viscous fluid, ejaculated from his nostrils, pools on the sheet like some cruel jokester's idea of semen.

"Damn," he says. "This is awful."

"It's not as if we expected anything," I say. "At least now we've tried it." Viagra works by relaxing the nerves and increasing bloodflow, presumably to the male member, but in Sam's case the nerves relaxed in that secondary sex organ, the nose.

We have the mistaken idea that we will find a quick fix, something that will—presto!—restore Sam to the way he once was. To this end we have committed ourselves to working our way through the available aids for impotency, Viagra being the first. Much later I will learn, through an Internet group, that other post-prostectomy men have restored potency only gradually and by various regimens meant to promote vascular health. Viagra is taken nightly, and in a low dose, not for sex but with the hope of restoring nocturnal bloodflow, an approximation of the erections a healthy man has every night in his sleep.

A prescription is also required for the next aid on our list—a vacuum erection device, or VED—and this of course requires Sam to engage in bureaucratic dispute. "Yes, I'm sure I need it!" I hear Sam shout into the phone. The VED company did not receive the correct paperwork from the HMO. "You think I'd be asking for it if I didn't?"

The VED arrives by UPS. It comes complete with a Kelly-green travel case and an instructional video. "This'll be interesting," I say to Sam. For I've given myself over now to this strange way of the body. These last, gynocentric months it was my turn to be the focus of attention. Sam was intent on satisfying me. But then he began to complain, and I as well, that he was outside our lovemaking, a mere observer.

The video features a man in a white lab coat sitting on a desk in a doctor's office. He welcomes us to "the family of vacuum erection device owners." Next we see attractive, active couples—playing golf, dining by candlelight—testifying that the pump allowed them to "reclaim their sex lives."

Back to our white-coated specialist, this time a close-up shot that shows his dimpled chin and a twinkle in his eye that may be flirtatious. He explains that the VED works by using a plastic cylinder to create an airtight vacuum seal around the penis, thereby forcing the blood necessary for an erection to flow in.

"Like the wine saver," I say to Sam. We have a pump that will draw the air from a partially emptied bottle of wine, to keep it fresh.

"Precisely," says Sam.

Next, we get a demonstration. A long crotch shot allows us to see a rather well-endowed Mr. X pump himself up—what we learn is called "creating an erection." Out of context, inside a transparent tube, the male member looks monstrous, a strange and bulbous creature. Next, the model demonstrates how to slip a tension ring around the penis base, to hold in the blood when the cylinder is removed—this, we learn, is for "keeping an erection." The tension ring can be worn for as long as thirty minutes, Mrs. X take note.

I am almost sorry when the video is ended. It was entertaining; something to mock. Now we must try, my husband and I. We are not as different from the couples on the video as I'd like to believe.

Sam, an engineer by inclination, is enthused about assembling the various parts.

"Do you want to be alone?" I ask.

"Are you kidding? Why would I want you to leave?"

"Privacy?"

I've heard women in the support group say that they feel estranged from their partner when he insists on pumping up solo in the bathroom. And I've read that men in cyberspace advise other men to practice alone until "you've got something to show her." What do I want? A part of me is curious. I want to see how the device works. But another part of me wants Sam to take care of things on his own. To be a man about his manhood problem.

But since he hasn't asked me to leave, just now it feels rude to leave him alone. I sit on the bed. Pants dropped, Sam screws the pump into the cylinder and then fits it around himself. He loses the vacuum seal, applies more lubricant to the cylinder rim, and then gets the suction tight again. Standing with legs apart and knees slightly bent, he gingerly pumps the lever. His face is scrunched up with concentration. He exudes anxiety. The seal breaks. Cursing, he must relubricate, begin again. This time he yelps in pain, twice, when the thing pinches him. He pumps again, falling into an easy rhythm, when lo and behold through the glass tube his member stiffens, like an injured bird taking flight.

We hold our breaths while he slowly removes the cylinder and attempts to adjust the tension ring. I am fully dressed, and more in the mood for jumping jacks than for sex, but if my partner has taken such pains to prepare himself, I figure I better be ready.

I undress and lie back on the bed. Here comes my relatively firm husband. I will do whatever he wants. He wants, he wants—

"Damn!" he says. "Damn, damn, damn."

Again, we are disappointed, and in a way that feels all too familiar. When we underwent infertility treatments to have Isaac, every month roller-coasted from an expectant, optimistic high to a crashing disappointment when once again I proved to be not pregnant.

We were hoping the VED would set things right. Apparently, the engineering is not sufficient. Or it's trickier to master than the video would have us believe. Sam practices with the pump several times over the next week, and each time, soon after he removes the cylinder, he droops back to his flaccid state.

The video posted a 1-800 number to call for twenty-four-hour telephone support, and I urge Sam to call it now, but he dismisses the idea with an offhand excuse.

"Why aren't you getting help?" I ask. "Are you going to be one of those men who won't ask for directions?

"It's not going to work," he says, and I hear the disappointment in his voice. "It's no use."

He packs the equipment back in its Kelly-green case. I take a deep breath. It's *his* body, I tell myself. This is difficult for him. But it's a breath to hold my anger in. For angry I am, not so much at my husband's impotency but that he's acting so impotent about tackling the impotency. I want him to take the bull by the horns, to act like a man, to show some balls. Learn to use the device. Find out what else you can do. If at first you don't succeed. . . All that macho stuff.

Again, we are mistaken in our thinking. We are looking at the situation in black and white: potent or impotent; up or down. We do not yet know that potency exists on a continuum, that many men pump up nightly for what they call exercise. But we have no real guidance. The HMO urologist merely writes out prescriptions, saying, "See if this will work." The support group meets only once a month. Surgeons are busy saving more lives.

Women treated for breast cancer have access to wigs, scarves, hats; to makeup advice; to insurance coverage for breast reconstruction—all presumably to make a woman feel better about her femininity. Men need a private place, as private and specialized as a cigar shop, one that sells vacuum erection devices and soft leather pouches for storing injectable paraphernalia; also, competing brands to Depends, which would put the damn incontinence aids on sale once in a while. An erection, we learn much later, is not an either/or situation. It's a bloodflow situation, a muscle situation, and an emotional situation.

Much later, I will write an article about our experiences with impotency for Salon.com. In response I will receive an e-mail from a Robert Young, who deserves special mention. At the age of sixty-one he was diagnosed with advanced metastatic prostate cancer, with a PSA of more than 1000, and given only months to live. He decided to create a Web site—Phoenix5, To Help Men and Their Companions with the Deeply Personal Issues Created by Prostate Cancer—that links to an online discussion group, Prostate Cancer and Intimacy (PCAI). There, one man writes his recipe for restoring potency:

I can only tell you what worked for me. I was 49, in great athletic shape, without vascular disorders, and few vices (no obesity, no smoking).

I started with VED 60 days post NS RRP and used it once daily for exercise for about 10-15 minutes. Later on I added Caverject about 2x/ week—these produced 30-minute erections. This was four years ago prior to the introduction of Viagra. I never lost length and normal function returned at about 21 months.

I would imagine results would vary greatly given age, physical shape, whether the impotence was permanent or not, etc.

If I were starting out again now, and my goal was exercise post—NS RRP, here is what I would do:

—Use VED daily like I did 4 years ago for exercise

—Try Viagra daily

—Try Viagra at larger doses for sex

—And if Viagra did not work initially (as it often does not for recent surgery patients) I would learn to use injectables.

This strategy would achieve the double objectives of physical exercise and psychological recovery.

A woman wrote in, complaining that her husband made love to her now out of what she felt was an intellectual obligation, only to satisfy her. I was interested in this topic, too, for I felt that things between Sam and me were heading in this direction. A man wrote back:

> Sex is no longer as fulfilling physically
> for me as it has been for most of our 51 years
> of marriage. But the sense of fulfillment,
> joy, bliss that overcomes me when I make love
> to Gwen is certainly more than intellectual. I
> would call it spiritual, or heartfelt. We have
> blessed memories of the fireworks, yet in our
> 70s stillness & peace are more important than
> excitement.

Sam and I have set ourselves this goal, of getting him to get it up. But maybe our goal is the problem. Maybe our goal should be how to get that fulfillment, joy, and bliss. Is there an exercise we could do for fifteen minutes each evening to keep us heart to heart?

~~~~~

It's December 1999, and Y2K paranoia is palpable. Friends are talking about buying a generator, stockpiling food and water, even leaving the country. Will anyone be alive on the earth in the new year?

Sam's and my Y2K plan is to evacuate our house in Cambridge for Sonia and Bruce's small mansion in Medford. We load our car with cake and gifts and Isaac's portable crib. Medford— where Santa and his sleigh climb the roof in colored lights, people leave their doors unlocked, and there are no cafés, only coffee shops.

We find Bruce in the kitchen, ladling juice over a twenty-pound roast. I sniff the buttery air. I lift pot lids: mashed potatoes, peas with white onions, Yorkshire pudding. Sam sets the wine bottles he's brought on the counter, slips off their fitted paper bags. "Aaah," says Bruce, who hails from Great Britain, "you've brought the good stuff."

"Noo-noo," says Isaac, pulling at my leg.

"You want noodles?" says Sonia. She opens a cupboard and out spill voluminous bags of rigatoni, penne, spaghetti, linguini, fusilli, orechiette, capellini.

"Costco again?" I ask.

"Y2K is a good excuse," she protests. "Did I tell you about the paper I'm working on?"

"I want all the noo-noos," says Isaac.

Quickly, I separate two packages from the pasta stash and slam shut the cupboard door on the rest. "Choose one," I say to Isaac. "The big noo-noos or the long noo-noos."

"I want to write about Costco as an American place of worship," continues Sonia. "The belief in abundance and replenishment. Outsmarting the market . . ."

"Don't forget the electronic import angle," says Bruce.

"How's your DVD player?" asks Sam.

"I always feel like I should have four or five kids to shop there," I say.

"Big noo-noos!" shrieks Isaac. "Noo-noos now!"

Sonia puts the water on to boil. I take Isaac's hand. "Let's go throw Socrates and Amy down the stairs," I say. Socrates and Amy are two giant stuffed gorillas that stand guard at the end of Bruce and Sonia's bed.

We drink and eat and drink some more. We chase Isaac through the echoing, unfurnished rooms until he is tired enough to fall mercifully asleep in his portable crib. We congregate in the room that Bruce calls the entertainment suite, which contains an oversized television set and two green-cushioned couches—one for each couple.

Bruce and Sonia. Sam and Karen. All of a sudden, relationships feel so simple. Sam or I select a movie from the shelf and the other one starts up the remote control. Across the room nestle Sonia and Bruce. I stretch out beside Sam. He nuzzles my cheek. Let the wind whip the windowpane. Let the world disappear. I have a warm companion to keep close. I have friends who offer abundance and replenishment. A story to watch. Tonight, which could be our last night on earth, we seek out only comfort and ease.

The next morning, I wake in a blue-painted room. Light streams in the uncurtained window. On the pillow beside me, hair as rumpled as a boy's, is Sam. I sit up in bed, blankets pulled to my chin. A car drives by outside. A dog barks. Then, silence, except for Sam's unhurried breathing. How many breaths have he and I taken together by now? Trillions of times, our lungs have expanded and contracted together. Zillions of times, our hearts have beat together. This morning, marriage feels so simple. I watch as he turns his head, slowly opens one azure eye. "Hey," I say. "Happy New Year. It's safe to wake up now."

The world is still here and it's full of sales. One bright cold morning in January, I set out for the nearest Victoria's Secret. As soon as I enter the pink and powdered vestibule I read the screaming signs: CLEARANCE. My blood begins to race, and whether this is in response to the inherent soft-core erotics of the establishment or simply in anticipation of getting a bargain is difficult to discern.

Women of all shapes and sizes are milling around the two center tables where the clearance lingerie overflows plastic bins, straps twisted around underwire, silk brushing satin. I meander over to the bin that's marked what I know to be my bra size: 38DD. I finger an item stitched from a faux Kandinsky print and I think of Sam. "Modern woman commodified as modern art," I can hear him say. He will use his joking, ironic tone, and I will feel the warmth from his body. I will be curvy and plumped, cleavage revealed.

And then I correct myself. Past tense. I *felt* the warmth from his body.

Part of what propelled me today, I will not deny, is the urge to spiff myself up for Sam. Although never before has lingerie played a significant role in our mating dance, lodged deeply somewhere is the hope and belief that I can make myself over for him; that the right panties, if not the right prescription, will restore his desire.

If sex is all in your head, Sam's and my heads have become filled with the memory of recent mechanical failures. His touch dampens rather than fires my desire. And lately his hygiene habits . . . Well, let's say it's my turn to complain about domestic details. Sam doesn't like me to talk about this, but he's taken to leaving his plastic diaper—overnight protection—on the bathroom floor. It lies there, voluminous and white, smelling faintly of urine, and I have to step around it to get into the shower. When I try, tactfully of course, to tell him that not only does this habit irritate me, but it erodes further the tenuous erotic connection we have these days, he gets angry. "Why are you focusing on details? Don't you understand what I'm going through?"

I say no more. It's difficult to sort out when I am supposed to stand by and be supportive, and when I am supposed to stand up for my own rights. Especially as it's painful for me as well to witness his intimate humiliations.

Remembering the soggy diaper incident now, I feel angry in an energizing sort of way. Why should I be the one to take responsibility for turning him on? Isn't he the one who's shutting me down?

"Excuse me," snaps a chesty woman with red-painted lips and hair growing black at the roots.

I step back. I am in her way, musing over the brassiere bin. And then my practical, bargain-hunting side takes over. I make my choices quickly. Laden with satin, I search out a dressing room.

For the first time in my life I find that the cup size is too large. The faux Kandinsky offers not enough support, too much room. When I ask the salesgirl to take my measurements, she loosens the tape from around her neck, wraps it around my bust, and I am surprised to find that I have come down a size.

"Women change," she says.

"Could it be from breastfeeding?" I ask. No lactation specialist ever mentioned this.

"Yes," she nods, "no question."

I know that many women would not welcome being downsized in the chest, but as for me, I am quite happy. By age eleven, when I still lived in the dreamy world of tree forts and Laura Ingalls Wilder books, I was already pretty large on top. My mother took me to a type of shop that is now nearly extinct. Nettie Greens, it was called. The saleswomen stood behind the counter with pins in their teeth. They prided themselves on giving a "good fit," and to this end they thought it their duty to pinch and press, to appraise. I stood in the dressing room breathing in my own clammy sweat. Again and again the matrons returned with larger and larger sizes. My body was burgeoning and could not be contained. The afternoon would never end. I would never fit.

All this comes back to me as I stand alone in the cool pink and white changing room at Victoria's Secret. It comes back to me, and then it vanishes for good, I think, like mist dissolving. In the mirror, today, I see with some irony and regret that just when I am old enough for the skin under my arms to begin sagging, my breasts have finally ceased to be such a weight. Ah, time: I am so much more confident in my own skin than I was when I was eleven.

Bin 36D is brimming with merchandise. Decisively, I pluck black, white, and a daisy decorated. I can feel the heat of my anger now, in my chest, traveling down to my hips and up to my brain. Here I am, in the prime of my life, the sexual peak, the romantic scales of my youth fallen from my eyes, the angst of my reproductive years almost behind me, only to find myself partnered with a man who—unintentionally, regrettably—has stripped me of my sexual self. My husband made a bargain to trade sex for his life, but that life is becoming colorless, for me as well as for him. I march right over to the panty bin. Here is mauve; here is taupe; here is maroon; here is peony. Colors meant to accentuate skin.

If I am working things through by shopping for lingerie, Sam proves to be an even more confident consumer. It is February 2000, market watchers take note, and Sam's stocks are rising. His portfolio is muscular and firm. He decides to repair his injured masculinity by purchasing that time-honored cliché of male prowess, a sports car. Not the extravagant Porsche he covets, but what he calls a poor man's Porsche—an Audi TT. Silver and sleek, it sits on the tar of our drive. February 2000, car enthusiasts take note: Ten years of precision engineering are revealed in its making. Several times each day, Sam walks around the car for the sheer pleasure of admiring its perfect lines. He takes it up Route 2 and steps on the gas. Please, I pray, knowing mine to be a foolish wish, let the car make him happier.

We go out for dinner, we two—no longer young, no longer new—to Blue Ginger in Wellesley, which is a good half-hour away. My husband wants to drive. He whom I have seen torn and bloody opens the door for me like a gentleman I would like to get to know better. On the ride out he is cool and confident. He turns on classical music. He turns a knob and my seat warms. He turns another knob and I am reclining. He shifts gears; he mans the brakes. He asks me questions about my day, about myself, and I find that my replies are full and in earnest, confident of his interest.

And that night, when we return, he tries yet another sexual aid. Muse, it's called. "Time to amuse ourselves with Muse," says Sam. "Here we go."

Another instructional video, where a white-coated woman recommends the missionary position. Ice packs applied to the inner thigh, she advises, can bring down an erection should it last longer than four hours. Don't worry, she says. Up to twenty million men are affected by ED.

Sam unwraps the foil pouch and removes the plastic applicator with its medicated pellet. He cringes as he inserts the thin plastic tube into his penis head. "Not bad," he says. "If it works."

Again, we wait to see if the drug will take. We could be fondling and fooling around, but our focus has shifted so that we are after one thing only. Back and forth, back and forth across the ten feet of our bedroom floor walks Sam, like a man determined to get somewhere—but where?

Because of course nothing happens the way it is supposed to happen. In fact, nothing happens at all. This time we're not even disappointed. We expect nothing. I am already in bed, the covers pulled up, looking forward to plowing through a big, fat book.

At the next support group meeting I exchange hellos with the other wives. We know each other's stories now. Holly is trying to convince her husband to let her accompany him to the medical appointments. Abigail's husband just went on injections. I notice new things tonight about the men: how their faces redden with hormone-induced hot flashes, how the eyes of the newly diagnosed are pinpricks of terror.

In the women's group, I relate Sam's failed experiments.

"Viagra hardly ever works," says Abigail with disgust. "I don't see why they even bother to prescribe it."

"Drug companies," says Nance.

"Joe couldn't handle the pump, either," says Holly. "Too complicated."

"There's always injections," moons Jeannie. "Is he ready to try them yet?"

"I think so," I say. "I think he's getting to that point. I think he's less squeamish. I'll suggest that he make an appointment with Goldstein."

There's a new woman here tonight. She is younger than the

other women, my age, mid-forties, and she tells us that her fi-
ancée has just been diagnosed and they are trying to decide on a
treatment plan.

"We want this behind us by the wedding this July," she says,
as if trying to convince herself that this is possible.

Around the circle, women nod, but skeptically.

"We're not even married, yet," she says. "We have a passionate
thing going."

Around the circle, more heads nod.

"The thing is, it's hard to know which way to go. The radiation guys advise radiation. The surgeons advise surgery. The seed
guys advise seeds."

"Surgery is the sure way to go," says Jeannie. "I'm sure glad
that gland is out."

"Surgery," says Holly.

"Surgery," says Nance.

"We've talked to some guys who did surgery," says the new
woman. "And they're not so happy with the complications.
They're pretty mad about losing it."

As I listen to this newcomer, I suddenly realize what an old-
timer I am in this disease. And I find myself wanting to tell her
about my experience.

I tell her about Sam's radiation almost ten years ago, which
had no complications, except for the maddeningly rising PSA.
Quality of life is what everyone talks about when it comes to
complications, I say, but no one mentions the lowered quality of
life that PSA anxiety brings. The lowered quality of life when you
are constantly afraid of imminent death. The lowered quality of
life when you don't dare think of the future. The lowered quality
of life when you are always waiting, expecting the worst. I'm a recent convert to surgery, I say, *despite* my husband's problems. Life

is better now than it was then, I say, and mean it. What I don't add, and try not to think about, is that cancer does return in an estimated thirty percent of men who have had undetectable PSAs immediately following a radical prostectomy.

Tonight, when we join the men in the auditorium, Rob, the men's group facilitator, announces that the men have something to say to us women. Collectively they've devised a list of questions. Things they need to know that they're afraid to ask.

We circle around like wagon trains camped on the prairie.

Rob's hands shake as he reads from a single sheet of paper.

How important is penetration?

Is there something you need from me that I'm unaware of?

How much sexual interest do you have?

Should I prepare (injection, vacuum pump) before or after we agree on sexual relations?

How much does it bother you that I take time out to prepare for sex?

What do we need to do to show you that we love you? ✦

12

EVER AFTER

Late one night I hear Sam answer the phone and say, "No! No! Oh no!"

His brother Alan is calling from Israel. Alan's ex-wife, mother of his three children, has been murdered by her lover, who then killed himself. The two of them were found lying in blood in her apartment, the pistol on the floor.

Now it is Sam's turn to help his brother. Coincidentally, he is scheduled to fly to Israel this very week to visit a friend of thirty years, Eva, who is being treated for advanced ovarian cancer.

Gallows humor is now in vogue. "Two simultaneous tragedies saves on plane fare," says Sam. "How convenient. Cancer and murder in one trip."

Truly, he is honored to be a source of strength and comfort. Alan and Eva turn to Sam, now, as someone who understands crisis. In the days before he leaves for Israel he is on the phone constantly, consoling his nephews and niece, listening to his brother recount more details: she was trying to leave her boyfriend of ten years, the gentlest guy, and somehow he snapped, people do. Sam, who lost a wife so long ago that she is no longer a palpable presence—and he is no longer the man she knew—can listen to his brother talk about his distress and grief. Can listen to his brother talk about the kids: one in the army, one in college, one working. Now he is their only parent. He hopes he can do it. He hopes they will not be scarred. *He* is scarred.

And Sam is advising Eva on second opinions, researching doctors in the States, comparing treatment plans, talking to her grown son.

"I feel *useful*," he says to me. "This is something I can do."

I no longer feel that fate has singled me out with Sam's illness. I no longer feel overwhelmed by its tragic proportions. Now, when I talk with someone I know, especially if they have reached a certain age, I almost expect to hear about a tremendous loss: a child died, a sibling killed, a ten-year illness, orphaned at fourteen, abused at five. Now, when I hear about loss, I see the gifts people receive when they plumb their grief and come up transformed: compassion for others, sensitivity to nature, soulful art, generosity, deep love. I see the courage people possess after they've weathered a personal crisis. Often, they are no longer afraid to write the book or take the journey or live as they choose. They know how to listen to the wind that comes down from the hills and rattles the windows at night. How to cook a simple meal of root vegetables and trout and taste each morsel. They have learned how to cherish.

When Sam returns from Israel, we go for our long-awaited appointment with Dr. Irwin Goldstein, the erectile dysfunction specialist reputed to be the best. The waiting room is windowless and small. We wait for what seems like a long time with nothing to read but months-old issues of *Car and Driver* and *Antique Mart*. Finally, we are called to see a psychologist (strange, because Sam's impotency is clearly physiological rather than psychological) who merely listens to Sam relate his entire medical history before waving us on to the great Goldstein himself.

"Good to meet you," says Goldstein. His handshake is hearty and warm. His office is happily messy, filled with sports trophies his kids have won and photos of himself on boats. He gets right down to business. "Let's see how you respond to my cocktail."

Four years earlier, I was the one who had to self-inject. In vitro fertilization requires daily shots; hundreds by the time I conceived. I was afraid and then I learned not to be. Now it is Sam's turn.

"Is there a possibility they won't work?" I ask. All this time the shots were our ace in the hole. Worst scenario, you'll do the shots, was what we've said. Besides, from what Jeannie reported at the support group, I was curious about the hours-long potential in my man.

Now Goldstein's and Sam's eyes meet. "They often do work," Goldstein says carefully.

In fact, this is not Sam's first shot at the shots. Six short weeks ago, before the murder, Sam went to New York to meet Alan, who was in town for a conference, representing the Tel Aviv branch of the computer company for whom he works. While in New York, Sam visited Dr. Eid, the ED specialist then at Sloan-Kettering. Sam hasn't told me much about the visit. Only that when given the standard dose of prostaglandin, he did achieve a rock-hard erection, but one that was terribly painful. A second shot brought him down.

We learn that post-prostectomy patients often have a kind of allergic reaction to prostaglandin. Dr. Goldstein is known for his art in mixing various drugs and dosages; today, the idea is to try alternatives to prostaglandin.

I accompany the men across the hall to the closet-size examination room. Sam lies back on the paper-covered bed. Goldstein presses Sam's penis between his fingers like a butcher weighing so much flesh, makes one quick jab with a needle, and then milks Sam a couple times to spread the medicine.

I stand in a corner, sweating in this overheated room, unable to remove my winter coat. Sam stands before the exam bed, a tiny bead of sweat on his nose.

Goldstein gives us a quick, appraising glance. "You two be okay for a bit? Be back in twenty minutes."

"What about my pants?" says Sam. "Up or down?"

"Six of one; half dozen of the other," says Goldstein. He waves his hand. "Suit yourself."

Laboriously, Sam pulls up his jeans, zips and buckles. "Gives me a little more dignity," he says.

We wait. The office is hot and dimly lit. The walls appear to be caving in, making the room narrower and narrower. My throat is parched, my tongue thick in my mouth. I cannot talk. I cannot move my arms to unzip my coat. Sweat oozes down the side of my torso. Sam seems far away, a man that I hardly know. His skin is sallow, his mouth turned down. He bends to touch himself. "Nothing yet," he says. "Nothing yet."

Seven times more, Sam makes a pilgrimage to Goldstein's Friday morning walk-in clinic. Various dosages and combinations are tried. Each time, before leaving, Sam says, "Don't expect anything. But if I come rushing home . . ."

"I'll be ready."

Each time Sam returns with his head down. The results are scant and insufficient. Goldstein has nothing left for him to try.

We are more or less at the end of the line for treatments. We've heard that Viagra is to be available as an injectable, but that possibility exists in the uncertain future. And we know that a penile implant is an option, but really, we are skeptical about further surgery in an area on Sam's body that has been repeatedly insulted by intrusions—radiation and then surgery. When Sam talks to Goldstein about an implant, he gets vague answers. The database for implant surgery on men who have had a salvage radical prostectomy is practically nonexistent. In any case, the recovery period after an implant might last three months. We're not willing to weather more surgery just now, especially when no one can predict how things will turn out for Sam.

Sadly, we are beginning to reconcile ourselves to Sam's more or less permanent impotency. Another way of saying this is that we are no longer trying or hoping that he will get it up again. This is who he is now. It's a loss. I grow quieter and quieter. I am trying to accept this altered man. I too must change.

I read a book by Susan Bordo called *The Male Body: A New Look at Men in Public and in Private.* Bordo writes cultural analysis. In a chapter titled "Hard and Soft," she argues that when we demand the penis to be hard, we 1) limit a man's pleasure to one part of his body, and 2) adhere to what she calls the cult of hardness. Men must be emotionally stiff, armored, and ready to perform. Essentially, says Bordo, when we talk about male potency what we really mean is for a man to become a dildo. And a dildo, as Bordo points out, and as Sam and I discovered, to judge from the fact that mine remains in a drawer—is unfeeling.

A soft penis, says Bordo, is about vulnerability, tenderness, sleepiness. Letting down one's guard. Becoming disarmed. *Feeling* rather than performance. I put down the book. Well, I think. If my husband could attain those enlightened qualities, I think I would be adequately compensated for his trouble.

You might say that I am merely rationalizing; that I am intellectualizing away a very real problem. That may be true. What's wrong, I say, with a little rationalization? We all rationalize to get through each and every day. Reframing allows me to make meaning of my problem.

My parents offer to take care of Isaac for the weekend. Friday afternoon, Sam and I drop off Isaac (and Rabbit and Misha Bear), hug my mom and dad hello and good-bye, and kiss our child one hundred times. We are off to New York.

For dinner on Saturday night, we meet Sam's old friend Rudolf, Sam's apartment mate in the Jerusalem apartment where the nightingale sang and women streamed in and out. One of the people Sam impressed me with that evening in Jamaica Plain when I cooked him artistic pasta and we first spent the night together, Rudolf the Rolfer lives in London now. He's in New York to see his therapist and clean out his mother's apartment. He's thinner than I imagined, and with less hair. He peers at Sam quizzically, as if searching for an expression that will bring back the friend he knew at twenty-five.

"Remember that woman Sarah?" asks Sam. We have finished drinking a bottle of wine and are sitting around the table. I enjoy listening to the two old friends reminisce. I'm seeing a new side to Sam tonight, the stoned-out, wild-haired guy who studied at the yeshiva until he found out he could pick up girls.

"Silly Sarah," says Rudolf. "She was crazy about you, Sam. Or just plain crazy. She used to sit at your feet and listen to you talk. Like you were the Messiah or something."

"Yeah," says Sam. "I heard she ended up in a psychiatric hospital. Those were the days."

"Whoever thought," says Rudolf, "we'd end up like this."

"Whatever this is," jokes Sam.

Sunday morning, we sleep late in the hotel's plush king-size bed. I am swimming up from sleep when I feel Sam's leg press mine. A tingling deep inside me. Perhaps because I am not fully awake, I am thinking this time not about shots or pumps or pills, but about pleasure. I want his skin against mine, and I press my leg back against his, the whole hairy scratchy warm length of his leg, where I can feel his blood flowing strong as I have not in a long time. I open my mouth to the spice-candy taste of his mouth, the ginger taste of his stomach. His hand reaches for me, and I feel again the purposeful strength in his touch. He strokes my thighs until I open, trembling and wet. His hands are two fish, dancing inside me, and his mouth is on me too, and for the first time since his operation I feel we are here together, feeding and, yes, desiring each other. His breath quickens. I place my hand on his shoulder and feel the vein throb. He turns in the bed so I can touch his silky soft penis and he moans with pleasure. I am giving and he is taking; and then I am taking and he is giving, and we are traveling together again, and it is lovely, lovely, lovely, and when I break he is there, too.

We doze a little in one another's arms.

This morning we have found a middle ground between hard and soft. A place where we can connect in pleasure. A place that relies neither on the stiff rod of pornography nor on flaccid, self-abnegating defeat.

I sigh, a tiny sigh that wakes up Sam. "Happy?" he murmurs.

I burrow my mouth on his arm so he will not have to doubt my muffled yes.

And then we know what we must do. We shower, we dress,

and we eat a sumptuous breakfast downstairs in the lobby while a pianist picks out old show tunes.

We take a cab uptown, to the Torneau building. Tick tick tick tick sounds the giant gray clock above the door. Tick tick tick sounds the thousands of watches in their velvet cushions. At this time last year we barely allowed ourselves to think ahead one week, two weeks. Now we can believe in keeping time together. We can believe in a lifetime of our two hearts ticking side by side.

We select beautiful, indulgent watches. For me, a square-face bracelet watch. For Sam, a Rolex.

I write these words in western Massachusetts, at the foot of the Berkshires, in late October, the foliage at its glorious peak. I am here by myself, for a week, and it is heavenly. One afternoon I go for a drive. I relish the fact that I do not have to listen to news bulletins (Sam's passion) or *Stuart Little* on tape (Isaac's passion). I can listen to what *I* love—the silence. I could easily drive and drive, it occurs to me. I could simply leave: west through Pennsylvania, Ohio, west to California. But what kind of woman would I be then? And how lonely I would be.

I drive through the little towns of Ashfield, Greenfield, Montague, Gil. I pass cows, silos, and maple sugar farms. Today, I need miles and miles of silence. I drive over hills that are gentle and rolling, beautiful rather than sublime, the kind of landscape of which one does not tire, for it is sustaining and kind. At its best, life with Sam is like this. The ash and the oak and the maple are all vibrant gold and auburn and red, bursting with color that is most intense and nuanced before the leaves fall.

Our life together is like this, too. I am lucky, I think, to be partnered with a man who understands my need for solitude and for connection. Again and again he will let me go and take me back, let me go and take me back, a rhythm as reassuring as the tide. A man who tells me, when I call home, "Isaac and I had a long talk today. We agreed that in a perfect world you could eat ice cream at any time of day or night. In the real world we live in, you can't eat ice cream before supper."

The real world we live in. The one I am learning to inhabit.

Being parents of a young child demands that we live more fully in the moment. As it turns out, this is a good discipline for living with a chronic illness, potentially life threatening. Caring for Isaac prevents self-absorption in our own woes. Living with Isaac means more rides on the merry-go-round and less listening to war reports. More Elmo Band-Aids for that miniscule scratch on the arm and less worry about PSA. More birthday cakes, trips to the beach, visits to the zoo. More hugs.

As for Isaac, the child we cherish, we can only hope that Sam's disease does not harm his spirit. We try not to dwell on mortality. We try to keep gloom at bay. We try to normalize life, to keep to schedules and routines. At the same time, we try to talk candidly about Sam's condition. Isaac knows that "Daddy had an operation and the doctors helped him to get all better."

He also knows that because of his operation, Dad sometimes has trouble peeing. Sam currently wears a Cunningham clamp during the day to keep from leaking—"a clothespin on my penis," says Sam—and a plastic diaper at night. We worried that this would impact Isaac's toilet learning. As far as we can tell, Isaac, like all children, simply had his own timetable and agenda: One week when he was three, he proudly mastered all the toilet skills required to join civilized society.

The real world we live in. The one I am learning to inhabit.

Because a routine test or exam—a mammogram or a Pap smear—can cause Sam undue anxiety, I have learned to inform him immediately of good news. When Isaac contracted the usual regimen of colds and flu, and I saw Sam go into high alert, I had to remind my husband that a simple stomach virus is not the same as a life-threatening illness. The times that Isaac falls down the stairs or knocks his head in play and cries hard, Sam has one hand on an ice pack while the other hand dials the emergency room. As a countermeasure, I tend to dismiss most injuries and illnesses as minor and temporary. I figure if I survived chickenpox, mumps, a broken ankle, scraped knees, rusty nails, infected toes, numerous viruses, and a tonsillectomy, so can my child.

Sam plans to stick around at least until Isaac's bar mitzvah, and we can only hope that it is to be. When Isaac hears mention of Sam's illness, he often responds by ministering to one of his beloved stuffed animals. To date, they have endured fire, drowning, being crushed by trucks, cannon attacks, shootings. Undoubtedly, his father's illness will figure into Isaac's life story, but what form that takes remains to be seen. He too is at risk for prostate cancer. Perhaps Sam's illness will make him sensitive to others with handicaps. Surely he will find a time to resent Sam's limitations, and to wish for a father with a clean bill of health. Perhaps, just perhaps, because of his father's struggle with "the essential male disease," Isaac will have a unique lens to view his own manhood, one that sees beyond the testosterone-driven, society-dictated, and allows him to experience his own, true self.

As for the real world Sam and I inhabit, it is a more peaceful one now. While we still struggle with order in the house, our domestic skirmishes are considerably less. Our house is professionally cleaned weekly now, and this disciplines me into the age-old middle-class occupation of getting the house ready for the house cleaner. The clutter does not get as wild as it once did.

To Sam's credit, he is more tolerant of disorder now that his body is better organized and no longer in crisis. He has learned to cast a blind eye to the mail stacks, the toy heaps, and the sinkful of dishes. I have gone away for four days, five days, and a week, for undistracted time in which to write. Each time, Sam has "done it all" and been gratified to find that one does not need mammary glands to take care of a small child or attend to meals, grocery shopping, and laundry. Here is his e-mail note:

Dear Karen,

Thanks for your sweet note letting me know you are in a good space. Your words warm even this stony old heart. Isaac and I are doing well together. I have just realized that it is no easier for you to take care of him alone than for me. A mind-awakening moment.

When I return, I find an exhausted husband, a scampering child, and a house in relative order. Isaac spends more time in Sam's lap than ever. Sam is quicker to respond when Isaac cries out. Isaac proudly shows me how he's mastered dressing and undressing himself. I have things I want to tell Sam, experiences to share. I've brought home a pumpkin pie, rubber stamps, and a green inkpad. Sam and I sit at the kitchen table, eating pie and drinking coffee, while Isaac stamps green rabbits hopping over stars.

Sam and I go out more together now, to Saturday night dinner and sometimes a movie, and for a few hours at least I meet again the smart, funny, warm man I fell in love with. We understand each other so much better now than when we first met. We are more forgiving than when we first moved in together. We have seen each other through despair and rage, fear and delirium, and those emotions, I think, make us part of each other. We breathe the same air, we eat the same food, and we sleep in the same bed. We have different opinions, different responses, and different ways of being in the world. We are two egos rubbing up against each other. Out of this, we have made a marriage.

Spring comes early the year after Sam's surgery. Isaac is three-and-a-half, golden-haired, and all questions. Do dinosaurs go into stores? What are necks for? When you were a kid, Mom, were you a boy or a girl?

"Time to host a Seder," says Sam. "We can do that now."

Indeed, it is time to give back. To give back to our friends and family from whom we received so much in a difficult time.

Sam inhabits the kitchen like a true believer. He chops and sautés like a man possessed. He stays up past midnight, scraping the marrow from bones. He cuts off the head from a glassy-eyed carp. No longer a habitué of fine Parisian chefs, he can care for himself now. Up to his elbows in batter, forming gefilte fish balls, he is at home. The kitchen smells like garlic and scallions and orange rind. He slow-cooks the brisket in wine. The kitchen smells of tomato and onion and beef. A man who believes in food—food as thanks, as pleasure, as community, as sustenance—he is ladling juice onto chickens and julienning carrots. He is popping corks. For this season of birth and renewal, he arranges a parsley sprig, peels horseradish, and roasts an egg.

I spread the white tablecloth. I set out the good china. I bring out the silver candlesticks. And then I am at my door.

I greet my father. He is carrying a covered dish and wearing a new shirt. He sees me now. He hugs me, tells me what a wonderful daughter he has.

I greet my mother. She hugs me too. She brings me a flow-ering begonia in a hanging pot.

I greet Aunt Gerdy, who also brings me a flowering begonia in a hanging pot, and who laughs a great laugh when she sees that my mother—her sister—and she have done exactly the same. I hang both gifts from the front porch. "How beautiful," I tell my mother and my aunt. And I mean it. I feel blessed with bounty.

I greet our old friend Willy, and his new bride Irina, the two of them rosy-skinned and glowing. I greet Sonia and Bruce, and their tiny baby Nigel, asleep in his car seat. I greet our new friends Lisa and Jack, and their spirited Sophia, who prances with delight when she sees Isaac, her playmate. I greet our friend and neighbor Philip, who came to impromptu suppers many times when Sam was fresh from the hospital and we needed a presence beside our melancholy selves to help us through the evening.

"Come in," I say to each arrival. "So glad to see you."

Our guests sit at the dining room table, the wide pine floor-boards gleaming with the light of early evening. Sam is at my side. Isaac scampers at my feet. Our house is full. Our table is laid. We sit. We read the old story out of Egypt: We were once en-slaved and now we are free. When we recount the plagues visited upon the Egyptians—frogs, vermin, darkness—for each of the ten we dip a finger into our cups to drip some of its red wine on our plates. We do this to remember affliction, to show how the woe of others takes away so many droplets from our enjoyment. I lick the wine that remains from my finger. I dare not linger on its supple, berry taste—I who have made meaning from personal crisis must learn now not to unduly savor its sorrow.

And then my husband Sam presents his great, gleaming plat-ters. We reach for our forks. We lift a morsel to our mouths. We have never tasted food like this. ✦

RESOURCES

American Cancer Society
1599 Clifton Road, NE
Atlanta, GA 30329
www.cancer.org
(800) ACS-2345

A comprehensive Web site for all cancer patients, with a section for prostate cancer. The American Cancer Society runs Man to Man, a network of local support groups for men with prostate cancer and their partners. Some areas offer Side by Side, a support group for partners of survivors, and/or a visitation program in which a trained prostate cancer survivor provides support to a man newly diagnosed.

CaP Cure
The Association for the Cure of Cancer of the Prostate
1250 4th Street, Suite 360
Santa Monica, CA 90401
(800) 757-CURE
www.capcure.org

Founded in 1993 by Michael Milken, CaP Cure is the world's largest private source of prostate cancer research, with many links to research, and offering Michael Milken's prostate cancer prevention cookbooks, *A Taste for Living* and *A Taste for Living World*.

www.cancerfacts.com
An online resource for cancer patients, their families, and caregivers, which delivers personalized medical information, including tools for decision making.

Malecare
www.malecare.com
(212) 673-4920

In New York City, Malecare currently runs more than twenty support groups for men with prostate cancer, two groups for spouses and children, a Spanish speakers group, and a group just for gay men and transgendered women with prostate cancer. All services are free and open to the public.

National Cancer Institute
Cancer Information Service
Building 31, Room 10A31
31 Center Drive, MSC 2580
Bethesda, MD 20892
www.nci.nih.gov
(800) 4-CANCER

Offers vital and well-accessible information on all aspects of cancer (specific questions answered in English and Spanish), a wide variety of booklets for coping with cancer, and a Physician Data Base Query with the latest information about treatment, prevention, genetics, and clinical trials.

National Prostate Cancer Coalition
1158 15th Street NW
Washington, DC 20005
(888) 245-9455
www.pcacoalition.org

Awareness, Outreach, and Advocacy are banner words for NPCP. A broad-based group that works with government and private industry on legislative issues that affect funding for prostate cancer research. Distributes *Smartbrief*, an online magazine deliverable to your e-mail address, and a Web site chock-full of medical information.

www.prostatepointers.org

Pointers follow to a variety of discussion groups to which one may subscribe. They include:

The Circle: Support for wives, families, friends, and significant others of men with prostate cancer.

SeedPods: A mailing list for those interested in brachytherapy (radioactive seed implants) as a treatment for prostate cancer.

IceBalls: Offers information and support to those interested in cryosurgery for prostate cancer.

Prostate Cancer and Intimacy: A frank and lively unmoderated discussion group for men and women, with a focus on the sexual/emotional issues surrounding prostate cancer.

www.Phoenix5.org

To help men and their companions with the deeply personal issues created by prostate cancer, Webmaster Robert Young has built a phenomenal site that should be a first stop for the newly diagnosed. Personal stories, medical information, and links to other sites are useful, comprehensive, and readable.

PSA Rising

www.psa-rising.com

A sharp, good-looking online magazine with all the latest news in prostate cancer treatments and research.

United States National Library of Medicine

www.nlm.nih.gov

The world's largest medical library and creator of MEDLINEPlus, an offering of articles, journals, dictionaries, and drug information by disease or ailment.

US TOO! International, Inc.

5003 Fairview Avenue
Downers Grove, IL 60515
Hotline: (800) 80US TOO!

www.ustoo.org

Modeled after Y-ME (support groups for women with breast cancer), US TOO! is the world's largest network of support groups for men and their families. The Web site lists contact details about local support groups for all states and some countries.